Repentance and Reconciliation
in the Church

REPENTANCE AND RECONCILIATION
IN THE CHURCH

Major Presentations Given at the 1986 National Meeting
of the Federation of Diocesan Liturgical Commissions

Doris Donnelly
Kevin W. Irwin
Kathleen Hughes, R.S.C.J.
Patrick R. Cooney
Editor: Michael J. Henchal

THE LITURGICAL PRESS
Collegeville, Minnesota

Cover design by MARY JO PAULY

THE LITURGICAL PRESS
Collegeville, Minnesota 56321

9	8	7	6	5	4	3	2	1

Library of Congress Cataloging-in-Publication Data
Repentance and reconciliation in the church.

    Includes bibliographies.
    1. Reconciliation—Religious aspects—Catholic Church—Congresses. 2. Penance—Congresses.
3. Catholic Church—Doctrines—Congresses.
I. Donnelly, Doris. II. Federation of Diocesan Liturgical Commissions. National Meeting (1986 : Portland, Me.)

BX2260.R45 1987   265'.6   87-3051
ISBN 0-8146-1572-4

Contents

Foreword

The sacrament of reconciliation is a sacrament in crisis. Indeed, the whole penitential discipline of the Church may well be in crisis. And the problem is not limited to the Church alone. Our whole society appears to have lost the ability to ask and receive forgiveness. Many have pointed to what they perceive as a loss of the sense of personal sinfulness. We are all witnesses to alienations and divisions in our families, the workplace, between old and young, between men and women, between people of different races or creeds or political philosophies, rifts even within the Church which seem incurable. Incurable, because we do not have a way to acknowledge, accept responsibility or, better, guilt, and then be forgiven.

Christ came into the world "to reconcile all things in himself by the blood of the cross," as we read in the first Eucharistic Prayer for Masses of reconciliation. It is that same ministry of reconciliation which God has entrusted to us (2 Cor 5:18). So when the representatives of diocesan worship offices and diocesan liturgical commissions met in Portland, Maine, in October 1986, we took as our theme: reconciliation. Obviously, as liturgists we had a particular interest in the effective celebration of the sacrament of reconciliation. But we also felt a need to deal with the issue more broadly—the alienations, hurts and divisions in our lives and in our world, and the elements and stages in the process of reconciliation. We also saw the need to look at the virtue of penance and the non-sacramental ways that have always been a part of the mystery of sin and forgiveness.

With our first speaker, Doris Donnelly, we began "at the beginning," as she puts it, "with hurt in the human family." She explores the process by which we deal with hurts. First, the hurt must be tested and owned. Then we must decide what to do about it: seek revenge, deny it, ignore it, or forgive it. If, in imitation of Christ, the choice is to forgive, then another process must take place. Mrs. Donnelly warns us against moving too quickly to a false reconciliation without real, prior forgiveness. In this regard she examines four "rituals" or exercises to help us move honestly from hurt to healing. The rituals proposed are rituals of lamentation, rage, unbinding, and conflict resolution.

Fr. Kevin Irwin helped us to look at the virtue and practice of penance in the non-sacramental sense: the classical triad of fasting, prayer, and almsgiving, and the role of the Word of God in the process of repentance and conversion. Influenced by what may be a sometimes misguided incarnationalism, these traditional practices, even when still kept, "can easily be reduced to pragmatic or utilitarian usages." In this way they can lose their power to bring about the radical openness to God which is conversion. In the context of the "eschatological edge and demand to our faith," they operate in three movements—purgation, formation, and transformation as good news—"because they bring us face to face with God in Christ as savior, redeemer, sanctifier, forgiver, mediator, reconciler, source of all life and source of all love."

"Disquieting" is probably an understatement when the issue at hand is an examination of the status quo of the sacrament. Sister Kathleen Hughes, R.S.C.J., minces no words in her analysis of the current situation. She first asserts that sacramental reconciliation is in actuality an extraordinary means of obtaining forgiveness in the lives of most believers, not the ordinary means Church documents sometimes presuppose. As such, sacramental reconciliation needs to be seen and celebrated as the conclusion to a process of turning away from sin, much as the Rite of Christian Initiation of Adults is. Two great obstacles stand in the way of the sacrament taking its rightful place: "ignorance and retrenchment." Ignorance, because few priests and even fewer penitents have the least idea what the attempted reform of the rite of penance called for. Retrenchment, because "a hankering after the alleged stability of preconciliar discipline, life, and thought" threatens to undo the reform before it even begins.

Bishop Patrick Cooney's contribution to the discussion offers a hopeful counterweight to balance off Kathleen Hughes's disquieting, however valid, reflections. After making his own summary assessment of the status quo on such aspects of sacramental practice as the decline in numbers approaching the sacrament, general absolution, first penance, confessions of devotion, and problems with each of the three forms of the sacrament, he asks, "Is there a future?" The hope for a future for the sacrament of penance is then shown to be contingent on our response to ten challenges. Some of these are of a more general nature, related to our understanding of the Church and symbolic forms in our ecclesial life. Others call for specific changes in our celebration and understanding of the sacrament itself, making it at once more communal and more of a process.

The Federation of Diocesan Liturgical Commissions, through the kind services of The Liturgical Press, shares these articles with you so that together we can get on with the task of "preparing the ground," as Bishop Cooney put it, so that sometime in the future the sacrament of reconciliation will be fully renewed in the life of the faithful.

MICHAEL J. HENCHAL

Portland Diocesan Liturgical Commission
Portland, Maine

Binding Up Wounds
In a Healing Community

DORIS DONNELLY

This is a story that starts at the beginning. It starts with hurt in the human family.

It begins with the story of Nicholas Gage, who left his position as senior investigative reporter and foreign correspondent for the *New York Times* in 1980 to explore the turbulent world of his childhood. [1] In particular, he went home to Greece to learn what he could about the death of his mother in 1948, when civil war was ravaging the country of Aristotle and Homer. It was a time when children were being abducted and sent to Communist camps inside the Iron Curtain. And it was a time when Gage's mother, Eleni Gatzoyiannis, a courageous woman who defied the traditions of her small village and the terror of the Communist insurgents, arranged for the escape of her three daughters and Nicky. For that act she was imprisoned, tortured, and executed in cold blood.

When Gage tracked down the facts of the story that mattered to him most, he learned brutal details of his mother's last days—how the soles of her feet swelled from continual beatings, how she was forced to march to the

11

site and then dig her own grave, how she faced the firing squad. Her "crime" was the seditious and revolutionary act of loving her children so passionately that she provided safe haven for them in America.

Layer by layer Gage uncovered the atrocities of the revolution and the details of his mother's death. Relentlessly pursuing every lead, he learned that the judge responsible for sentencing his mother to death was still alive. Gage arranged a meeting. The judge, named Katis, was aged and ailing, and the confrontation was entirely unsatisfactory. Katis blandly dismissed the charges of murder—so many were killed, who is to count? Katis challenged Eleni's innocence and oozed arrogance, with not a shred of repentance.

Gage seethed with a rage that knew no bounds. He had decided at the first meeting to avenge the death of his mother by killing Katis. To that end he vowed to confront him again, which he did four months later, when Katis and his family were vacationing in a rented apartment overlooking the Ionian Sea.

One day after Katis's wife, daughter, son-in-law, and two grandsons had left for the beach, Gage, knowing that Katis was alone, let himself into the apartment by opening the lock with a plastic card. He found Katis asleep in a chair pulled up to the picture window of the living room.

Katis did not stir as Gage stood over his body. Gage felt no pity for him, his age, or his helplessness, only hatred and revulsion. He had a gun tucked in the small of his back, but he realized that he could simply smother the judge with a pillow and leave. Katis's family would return to discover that he had died in his sleep. No one would suspect that he had been killed. Gage writes:

I stood staring at the man who had killed my mother for a few minutes, perhaps more. Then I turned around and walked out, closing the door softly behind me . . . I had found the perfect opportunity for killing him and I couldn't do it.

I have done nothing since leaving Igoumenitsa but ask myself why . . . I know it was fear that stopped me: partly fear of being separated from my children and setting in motion events that would continue the killing and the suffering into future generations. It was also something else: the understanding of my mother that I had gained in my examination of her life.[2]

During his search Gage learned of some of his mother's last words. To one friend she remarked on the good fortune of another friend in saving both her daughters and her own life, but she said nothing of hatred or revenge. When the town gossip, who had falsely accused Eleni, was brought to face her on the day of her execution, Eleni did not speak of the suffering of her torture but only of her desire to see her children one last time. And her final cry, before the bullets of the firing squad tore into her, was not a curse on her killers but an invocation of what she had died for, a declaration of love. "My children!" she said.

Alluding to heroines of Greek tragedies, Gage writes:

Unlike Hecuba, my mother did not spend the last of her strength cursing her tormentors, but, like Antigone, she found the courage to face death because she had done her duty to those she loved. Sophocles' Antigone tells the man who has condemned her to death [who happens to be her uncle and the king], "It is not my nature to join in hating, but in loving."

That was the nature of Eleni as well, and no one was able to destroy it by killing her. I was aware that if I had

killed Katis, I would have had to uproot that love in myself, purging myself of all humanity or compassion.

Killing Katis would give me relief from the pain that had
filled me for so many years. But as much as I want that satis-
faction, I've learned that I can't do it. My mother's love,
the primary impulse of her life, still binds us together, often
surrounding me like a tangible presence. Summoning the
hate necessary to kill Katis would sever that bridge connect-
ing us and destroy the part of me that is most like Eleni.[3]

Hurt in the human family. Not all of it is as extreme
as that suffered by Nicholas Gage, and a good deal of hurt
and its resolution is couched in more Christian language,
but his story will do, nonetheless, to teach us about the
pervasiveness of hurt in everyone's life, to speak of hurt's
aftermath, the problems that surround hurt, and the un-
even record in Christian experience for dealing with hurt.
The fact that we are able to inflict hurt on one another,
of course, is to speak of the presence and power of sin—
not an absolute power, mind you, but a power—and if
we find ourselves blocking out the dizzying sight of sin's
lethal and fearsome depths, all we need do is look behind
the headlines in the newspapers to violence in families or
violence between nations or the violence that an individual can inflict on himself or herself to recognize that the
subject is sin.

The story of Eleni and her son tells us that human hurt
is not gender-specific, which means that men suffer hurts
every bit as much as women; nor is any group immune
to hurt—bishops suffer hurt as much as busdrivers; nor
is hurt age-specific—children suffer hurts as much as adults
do, and occasionally, as in Nicholas Gage's case, there are
residual hurts which are not healed in childhood and which
then move unresolved through adolescence into adulthood.

The Gage family story also tells us that hurt has various sources. Sometimes we bring it on ourselves; sometimes, like Eleni and countless numbers of our brothers and sisters in war-ravaged countries, there are those who are innocent victims; sometimes we deserve some of what we get and are undeserving of the rest.

Nicholas Gage's story is also instructive when it comes to the process of dealing with our hurts. Gage identified his hurt and "tested" it so that he could be sure that his impressions tallied with reality. In his case the synchronicity between anguish and reality was painfully accurate: he will eventually have to forgive his mother's murderer. More proximately, he may need to come to terms with forgiving himself for his vengeful thoughts, and one day he may need to "forgive" God for allowing such freedom to creatures like Katis and for allowing them to betray their identity as God's children by preferring dark choices to light ones.

Once "tested," Gage "owned" his hurt and claimed it in all its goriness, and then decided what to do about it. He selected revenge, a popular choice among the wounded of the human race. His revenge was of the blatant and clear-cut variety. Some revenge that I have witnessed is more subtle—it goes within, and its net result is to kill the avenger and not the avenged in the long run, proving the truth of the old Chinese proverb that the person who pursues revenge should dig two graves. I have also known persons who enlist the aid of God in pursuing their revenge schemes and who pray for the demise, ill health, and death of the offender and all kinds of mischief on the heads of the offender's kin. The underlying assumption of this kind of prayer is that God will "do in" the aggressor for us when we have exhausted the means of revenge open to us.

Instead of avenging hurt, some persons choose to deny it, preferring pretense to truth. I am easily sympathetic to those who do not want to face hurt square in the eye, who do not want to deal with it, and who choose to run the other way. Others acknowledge that they are hurt but choose to ignore it, assuming that it will go away, much like a rash. Hurt does not work that way. It functions more like a wound that needs to be cleaned out and bandaged before healing can begin. To do otherwise—to patch a Band-Aid over a wound without cleansing it—is to leave ourselves wide open to infection and more serious problems further down the road.

There is one more thing one can do with hurt, and that is to forgive it (or to extend forgiveness when we are the cause of the hurt to another). What this means, in situations like the one described by Nicholas Gage and in countless other situations of greater or lesser gravity, is to defy the laws of common sense and reason. The act of forgiveness is so ludicrous in the face of injury that we need to be eternally grateful that Jesus not only preached but also practiced forgiveness. The crucifix is the ongoing acting out of what forgiveness means: to remain open and loving even when one is hurt. Jesus does that purely and lights the way to a remarkable form of existence when one buys into forgiveness and not revenge.

In this connection, Gage points to the healing agent of hurt when he unsentimentally but rigorously talks about love. However trivialized that word "love" may be, it leaves undiminished the gospel teaching which claims that love is the most formidable force in the world. It is capable of being battered, and even—heaven help us, as Good Friday reminds us—capable of being crucified, but capable as well of transforming and restoring wholeness to all who kneel in the shadow of the cross.

A great deal of confusion exists in our use of the words "forgiveness" and "reconciliation."[4] For me, the equation has three terms. The first is hurt, which needs to be identified, tested, and owned before we proceed to forgiveness, which is possible only by reaching to a power beyond us. Forgiveness demands that we look our hurt straight in the eye, that we assess the damage done to our psyches, our bodies, our spirits, and with all our wits about us choose—decide—will to forgive. That may sound preposterous, but only in that way is healing to be found. The third and final step of the equation is reconciliation, which is a bringing together of that which belongs together but which is apart. It happens only when forgiveness precedes it.

It is amazing how gifted we are at pretending in these stages. Our hurts are veiled, ignored, denied, suppressed, repressed, dismissed. An etiquette which suggests that conflict and hurt are inimical to the gospel message and must be avoided prevails in our churches—*especially* in our churches. There are times when we are polite to a fault, preventing each other from expressing the rituals of rage that need to accompany our suffering.

Nothing saves like the truth, and the truth is in short supply when we rush toward a reconciliation without pausing to forgive.

The lessons one may extrapolate from Luke's parable of the prodigal son are endless, but it seems to me that one of its wisest moments comes when the elder son meets with his father, whose behavior is paradigmatic of Yahweh's behavior, and says, equivalently, "I am hurt," "I will not fake a reconciliation," "I am not ready to forgive because

my wounds are so raw," "Forgiveness is not easy," "Forgiveness takes time." It is especially comforting that the
father in the parable—Yahweh—does not protest the
human response—the *healthy* human response—but instead invites to perfect forgiveness and celebration, reminds
the elder son that he is and always has been safely surrounded by love, and then waits for the process to complete its course. One might have the same hope for Nicholas
Gage. At the end of his account Gage has neither forgiven
nor been reconciled, but he has confronted an enormous
agony with courage. There are seeds of hope in the midst
of such tragedy. And there is power—the power of a
mother's love that cannot be quenched. The ripple effect
of that love surfaces at the most unpredictable moment
and strengthens Gage's resolve not to allow that love to
die but rather to determine the course of action of adult life.

A story like Gage's raises the question of whether we
do our catechesis and preaching from the wrong end, beginning with God's story before the human story is told.
Telling stories of human hurt and pain is a form of con-
nectedness that enables us to appreciate the lavish, uncon-
ditional, total, perfect love of God, so unlike the meager
way we do our forgiving.

Some Liturgical Approaches to Hurt

Gage's story prompts us to consider the climate in our
Church with regard to hurt and sin and with regard to
healing and forgiveness. In particular, are we creating a
climate in which people like Mr. Gage can give vent to
their anger, frustrations, betrayals, conflicts, pains, and
agonies? Are we creating a climate in which the truth of
our brokenness and sin can be spoken? My strong hunch

is that we are not doing this adequately (in some places we may not be doing it at all), and I believe that the time is long overdue to address this absence.

To this end, I believe that we need to respond to the pastoral task by introducing exercises or rituals that facilitate the healing process. Let us now look at four such rituals that could expand and strengthen the experiences of forgiveness and reconciliation at the heart of the sacrament of penance.

Rituals of Lamentation

The first of these exercises is a ritual of lamentation— the kind that shaped the experience of Israel and brought it to expression so that hurt could be dealt with.

It was Israel's style to see unflinchingly and to affirm without embroidery life as it comes, with its joys but also with its hurts, betrayals, loneliness, diseases, threats, anxiety, bewilderment, anger, hatred, and anguish. Scripture scholar Walter Brueggemann wants us to believe that this approach is antithetical to the antiseptic "one-sided liturgical renewal of today [which has, in effect] driven the hurtful side of experience either into obscure corners of faith practice or completely out of Christian worship into various forms of psychotherapy and growth groups."[5]

Israel was, if not more familiar, then certainly more comfortable with a pattern of rhetoric found in the Book of Lamentations and in the psalms of lamentation, in which the community without embarrassment addressed its greatest hurts to God. Brueggemann writes:

> Nowhere but with God does Israel vent her greatest doubt, her bitterest resentment, her deepest anger. Israel knows that one need not fake it or be polite and pretend in God's pres-

ence, nor need one face the hurts alone. In the dialogue, Israel expects to understand what is happening and even to have it changed. [6]

Think how reluctant we are to deal openly with one another, let alone with God, in areas of conflict. As a result, we repress our anger and hatred, "we muffle our cries of betrayal and absurdity, but even more acutely, with our failure of nerve and our refusal to presume upon our partner in dialogue, we are seduced into nondialogic forms of faith, as though we were the only ones here." [7]

By contrast, the faith expressed in the lament was nervy. Ancient Israel could face—and did face—predicaments with total candor and never doubted that they could be handled in dialogue with Yahweh. The lamentation begins by addressing Yahweh with bold confidence and culminates in grateful trust. Not only has the situation been changed, but the speaker's relation with Yahweh has been reaffirmed and solidified. It moves from situations of hurt to situations of potential transformation.

One of the clues to the success of lamentations is the hyperbole with which they were done in Israel: "Each of my bones aches"; "My mouth . . . my ears . . . my eyes all groan." The invitation to total release is salutary and gives way to tears or laughter, either one of which has possibilities of being a freeing experience.

Consider for a moment the practical and visual possibilities of this ritual within our own church communities:

—A community gathers to lament.
—A prayer like this one by Ted Loder opens the ritual:

Lord,
plunge me deep into a sense of sadness
at the pain of my sisters and brothers

inflicted by war, prejudice, injustice, indifference,
that I may learn again to cry as a child
until my tears baptize me
into a person who touches with care
those I now touch in prayer. [8]

—Perhaps individuals have been selected to tell their stories
of woe; perhaps the community has been invited to do
what in fact occurs in the Book of Lamentations: to name
their griefs alphabetically. One by one, in order, the community would come forward with their stories.

—Release of pain is expressed through song and prayer.
"Were You There When They Crucified My Lord?" comes
to mind as a possible hymn of lamentation. The repeti-
tion of the line "Sometimes it causes me to tremble,
tremble, tremble" might follow each lament, emphasiz-
ing the element of pathos and sadness surrounding the
pouring out of grief.

—A "Litany of Trust" closes the service—a trust expressed
to God for turning our lament around and freeing us from
its oppressiveness.

—Finally, *shalom* would be extended to all.

Such a ritual would say, first, that sometimes the pain
is unbearable and only a scream will do to express it; second, that grief and suffering are public and require expression within the community; and third, that when we
grieve or lament, there is need for a listener—an "ultimate"
listener who can transform the event into an experience
of wholeness.

It would not seem far-fetched for us to consider a ritual of lamentation in our communities to answer the needs
of hurting people who are aching to pull out all the stops
and make their pain known.

Rituals of Rage

The second ritual that might be incorporated into our liturgical practice is a ritual of rage.

Rituals of rage are corporate witnessings of outrage at injustice, and they, too, have roots in the prophetic tradition of Israel. But unlike the rituals of lamentation, which are litanies of personal grief, rituals of rage deal with complicity and collaboration in sin, and they call for the community to rage against these hurts that bruise the Body of Christ. Frequently these rages would be private griefs writ large, but they could also be political, social, or cultural.

A ritual of rage offers a range of imaginative possibilities: a rage against lies, a rage against tyranny, a rage against oppression. The Sojourners community in Washington, D.C., for example, rages with unrelenting regularity against hypocrisy in our government spending programs, and while their politics may or may not be your style, they effectively model the subject content for a ritual of rage. In another area, it might be interesting to see what would emerge if we encouraged women to develop effective rituals of rage expressive of their hurts and frustrations in the Church community.

Like rituals of lamentation, those of rage would have as their primary purpose a transformation of the emotions of anger and hostility so that energies could be channeled more creatively and less destructively. To rant and rail may be cathartic exercises, but they are inadequate if engaged in merely for that purpose. We rage not simply for the sake of hearing our own sound and fury but because of the need for our emotions to be cleansed so that a healing can take place.

A ritual of rage might take the following form.

—A community gathers because of a common hurt—a citywide vote against providing shelter for the homeless or an injustice done to an individual.

—A representative of the group (the leader) articulates the focus of the rage. The community gives its assent.

—Readings from Scripture (Isaiah or Jeremiah, perhaps) and a contemporary reading (from Martin Luther King, Jr., or Dorothy Day) are offered for inspiration and reflection.

—The words are juxtaposed with the particular rage expressed by the group in a well-crafted homily.

—Prayers are offered that destructive energy be transformed into creative energy and that peace replace feelings of hostility.

—Petitions offered from the group should include prayers for wisdom, strength, forbearance, and yielding.

—A resolution to take action to correct the injustice and the cause of the rage concludes the ritual.

A ritual of rage, like a ritual of lamentation, underscores the truth that there is a place for the emotions in prayer. The community gathered is a passionate community, a people of flesh and blood and spirit. Most important of all, however, a ritual of rage gets the message out that emoting is only half the story; the other half involves doing something to effect a shift in balance so that justice will reign again.

Rituals of rage are necessary statements on behalf of powerless groups whose voice has been reduced to a whisper, if not totally muffled. Rituals of rage are ultimately expressions of the human spirit that defies the odds and claims the possibility of new life from the ashes of lethal situations.

This may be the time to institute rituals of rage in our faith-communities to show how social action and liturgy are, in fact, two sides of the same coin.

Rituals of Unbinding

The third truth that needs to be reinstituted and remembered in the assembly is that we must be perceived as an unbinding community, not only as a binding one.

In conjunction with this, I was sobered recently by a comment made by Fr. John Catoir, the director of the Christophers, who wrote:

> After nearly ten years as the chief judge of a diocese marriage tribunal and five years as clergy personnel director during a period when 10,000 priests throughout the world were leaving the active ministry and now nearly seven years as the director of the Christophers, after having traveled around this country giving talks and listening to people . . . I have come to believe that vast numbers of Catholics have distanced themselves from the Church for a shocking reason: they perceive the Church to be unforgiving. It is the image they have received and apparently the one we unconsciously keep sending.[9]

I would like to believe that this image flows from a set of unconscious signals that we send out, and that we are not intentionally culpable, but I am not at all certain that this has always been the case. The sense that some persons have—and I have in mind here the divorced and separated, the divorced and remarried, the children of divorced parents, former priests or canonical religious, and gays—is that we intentionally and deliberately choose to disbar them from the fold, or that we accept their allegiance suspiciously and provisionally—in other words, that we keep them bound to errors, mistakes, and choices that they have made and from which we refuse to release them. Perhaps the time has come to consider unbinding what we have so effectively bound.

Our lead in the ministry of unbinding is none other than Jesus. It was he who initiated contact with persons who were bound to their failures and sins by the Pharisees. To those persons Jesus came as Liberator, and he effected an unbinding unprecedented in the Jewish tradition. The story of the cure of the paralytic underscores how surprised the assembled people were when Jesus unbound the paralytic from his illness as well as from his sins. In their hearts they murmured, "Why does the man talk in that way? He commits blasphemy! Who can forgive sins except God alone?" (Mark 2:7).

The tradition implicit in these thoughts reminds us that the rabbi could do one of two things with regard to sin: he could declare the promise of forgiveness to the whole community, or he could declare to an individual that his or her sins would be forgiven by Yahweh at the final judgment. It was not in the power of the rabbi to forgive the sins of an individual here on earth. That power belonged only to Yahweh. Yet Jesus seems to have taken this unbinding ministry upon himself with what his opponents perceived as unprecedented nerve.

Likewise, Jesus unbound the woman who interrupted the dinner party at Simon the Pharisee's house (Luke 7:36-50). Responding to her body language and her repentant gestures, Jesus declared her sins, her many sins, forgiven because she loved much. He unbound her from a disordered past and offered a clean slate for the future. Jesus also unbound the woman taken in adultery by separating her from her crime (John 8:1-11). He did the same for Zacchaeus (Luke 19:1-9).

Some interesting reflections for pastoral practice emerge from these stories. For example:

1) The emphasis that Jesus places on a healing ministry becomes extravagantly clear. When hurt is identified, Jesus zeroes in with laser-beam determination and offers an alternative to the status quo. Where people were paralyzed—and make no mistake, all the persons mentioned above suffered a paralysis—Jesus proposed a cure.

2) Jesus initiates the healing and forgiving process. If we take our clue from the story of the paralytic's healing, we note that Jesus does not wait for someone to ask for the needed healing but offers it unhesitatingly.

3) Jesus acts with confidence. What he says, he will and can do. He does not doubt his ability.

4) Jesus acts with power. Years of binding are broken: the strength of Jesus' words undoes quickly what it took years to do. Psalm 103 captures the drama: "As far as the east is from the west, so far does he remove our sins from us" (v. 12, Good News Bible). The decisiveness of the act is unmistakable.

5) In at least two of the unbinding stories—that of the woman at Simon the Pharisee's house and that of the woman taken in adultery—Jesus also does some binding of his own. It is worth noting how he does this.

In pastoral practice there seems to be much concern about how to correct wrongdoing, how to call sin a sin. For anyone interested in learning a thing or two, Jesus provides an approach to how binding is done honestly and at the same time compassionately. It is done so effortlessly that we may miss the event in the first of these stories, but Jesus bound Simon rather decisively. The fact that he bound Simon after he magnanimously unbound the woman was not lost on the dinner guests; certainly the point was not missed by Simon. Jesus is crystal clear about certain sins of omission (see Luke 7:44-47): You, Simon, did not kiss me. You, Simon, did not anoint my feet. You, Simon, did not love much.

The simple point is that Jesus is as effective at binding as he is at unbinding. But the binding is not done gratuitously. It is a binding done so that an unbinding can take place. It is a call to repentance so that after repentance a reconciliation can occur.

Imagine what those unbound by Jesus must have felt—exhilaration, restored self-esteem, relief, a sense of a new beginning after years of paralysis. With the power of that unbinding in mind, let us consider a rite of unbinding that might fit into our pastoral practice.

All of us have been bound by someone—or by ourselves—to some miscalculation we made or to some sin we committed, to some judgment or some decision we pronounced that we will never live down. Or we know where we have bound others—our children, perhaps, to live up to unreal ideals; or our friends or colleagues or superiors, to live up to unrealistic expectations. Or we feel bound before God and need to be set free. The community needs a reminder of these core human experiences of being bound and of binding others, calling to mind places, times, and people who glued us to our mistakes and the times we did that to others.

Both the bound and the binders need to be gathered for an unbinding ritual. The invitation is extended to us all, but special pastoral sensitivity must be shown to the marginalized, the rebuffed, the condemned, who are particularly bound.

—The community gathers, its members bound to one another

at the wrist or blindfolded or gagged. They may have asked to choose one of these options.

— The music for the ritual is something on the order of "Let my people go" or "Set me free," accenting the fact that the assembly is bound.

— The prayers suggest the powerlessness of the members of the community to unbind themselves and their need for a deliverer.

— An unbinding takes place, symbolically through the celebrant or by having the members of the community unbind one another.

The members are called to believe, as the paralytic was called to believe, that they are healed and whole and new, that Jesus Christ has given them new life.

Such a ritual would reinforce the message that we were not meant to live as bound persons, that we need someone to set us free, and that it is a freeing experience to be unbound and unconditionally forgiven. A parallel message exists for the binders to loosen up on unrealistic expectations, to unbind in those places where such an act needs to be done. The new result for the community is a gathering of freer individuals to proclaim the good things God has done for them.

Unofficial Rituals of Conflict Resolution

Finally, we have to rethink our primary rituals of reconciliation. This will not mean refashioning any of the options connected with the new rite of penance. Nor will it involve refocusing the Eucharist as the major sacrament of reconciliation, although that is closer to what I am aiming at.

The primary ritual of reconciliation in our community happens (or fails to happen) in relationships in families, parish councils, Catholic schools, diocesan agencies, chanceries, rectories, convents, homes, and any mixture of these long before we come near the reconciliation room, confessional, or altar.

How the Church reconciles or fails to reconcile its dissenters, prophets, progressives and regressives, men and women, clergy and laity, First World and Third World members, young and old, doves and hawks—*its own*—is where the credibility of the Church lies. Is there anyone who thinks that we are effective agents of reconciliation through the sacrament of penance if we do not model peaceful conflict resolution in our own Church family?

Our effectiveness—or ineffectiveness—in these prior rituals of reconciliation may explain the credibility gap the Church is experiencing as the agent of reconciliation it is meant to be. Could it be that we are not perceived as being very able reconcilers when there is trouble in our own backyard?

Of course, there are many who believe that the Church is not the place to deal with conflict. The perception among some is that conflict is antithetical to ecclesial etiquette, that it is abnormal (hence sinful) behavior, and that when one engages in conflict, one is immediately enmeshed in a no-win situation. The gospel has it the other way around, it seems. Jesus recognized conflict as part of ordinary life, and when it arose he dealt with it. [10] It was neutral ground for Jesus, apparently, not to be judged as sinful or as prized. What Jesus managed in dealing with conflict, however, was to move it away from a win-lose situation to a win-win situation. The Christian community must see reconciliation as a win-win situation, and it must see this modeled in Church conflicts on the front pages of the national press. To see anything else is to seriously compromise the vision of the Church as reconciler in today's world. If the perception is that we are unable to reconcile differences, or that we do so through a power based on fear and domination, our efforts at encouraging the community to be reconciled will falter.

One other perception may stand in the way of acknowledging the Church as an effective reconciling agent, and that is the sense that some have that the Church operates on a double standard. They ask whether the Church preaches against sin but excuses sin in some quarters when its own interest is at stake. For example, does it denounce sins of sexual excess in some corners and look the other way when those sins involve its own? We are talking about perceptions here, and when the perceptions do not tally with the facts, the official Church must set the record straight. Otherwise it may appear that the perceptions have merit of their own. Of course, there is much to be gained when the institutional Church identifies itself as both holy and sinful. That kind of humility and honesty would go a long way in inspiring others to do the same sort of authentic reckoning.

What we need, above all, is a community in which we can all tell the truth, in which there are no cover-ups, in which we can be ruthlessly honest. We are sinners. We need a Church in which the climate is accepting and supportive enough for the call to conversion to pierce us all. Popes and plumbers, secretaries and senators, liturgists and lawyers, accountants and astronauts—we all need to drop our masks and admit that we are all in the same boat as greedy, manipulative, lustful people, and that the grace of God alone is able to save us from ourselves.

We are imperfect healers in the service of the perfect Healer, who encourages us to lament, to grieve, to rage, to unbind, and to be reconciled in the pews before reconciliation is celebrated on the altar. He is our leader to the truthful way of being fully human and fully alive.

NOTES

1. My reporting of this story is taken from Nicholas Gage, *Eleni* (New York: Ballantine Books, 1984).

2. *Ibid.* 622–23.

3. *Ibid.* 623.

4. Doris Donnelly, *Learning to Forgive* (Nashville: Abingdon, 5th ed. 1986).

5. Walter Brueggemann, "From Hurt to Joy. From Death to Life." *Interpretation* (Jan. 1974) 4.

6. *Ibid.*

7. *Ibid.* 5.

8. Ted Loder, *Guerillas of Grace: Prayers for the Battle* (San Diego: Lura Media, 1984) 15.

9. John Catoir, "Is the Church Unforgiving?" *America* (Jan. 19, 1985) 47.

10. There are several examples of this, but one can see the win-win model of conflict resolution done effectively in Jesus' encounter with the Canaanite woman (Matt 15:21-28).

The Good News of Repentance and Conversion

KEVIN W. IRWIN

In his book *The Challenge of Jesus*, John Shea writes:

> Perhaps the most neglected line of the Gospels is the injunction of the Matthean Jesus, "Do not look dismal." The Christian religionist has managed a popular reputation, not entirely unearned, for being glum. He is often serious to the point of morbidity and comes across as a tightkneed naysayer. Almost everything is "no laughing matter." Jesus' challenge to repent has been transformed with a certain amount of dark pleasure to a call to wallow in guilt. Sin lurks on the underside of every joy and we can never be too careful . . . . This caricature is reinforced by a story Groucho Marx tells. Groucho is standing on a street corner in Montreal. A priest who is passing by recognizes him and says, "Mr. Marx, I want to thank you for bringing so much joy into the world." The eyebrows arch and Groucho strikes, "And I want to thank you, Father, for taking so much joy out of it."[1]

I begin with this quintessential Shea description and "story" because I fear that the topic can seem to combine things that are so serious that they can appear to be dismal correlatives—repentance and conversion on the one hand, "good" news on the other. This is especially true since we will be concerned with ascetical practices that are meant to foster conversion—fasting, prayer, almsgiving, and prayerful meditation on the Word of God.

Unfortunately, for too many of us, to speak of repentance and conversion is to speak of the "bad" news of Christianity and of the things we would rather not have to "give up" or "face up to" in order to be followers of Jesus. Rather, the title of this article states precisely what I want to argue, namely, that repentance and conversion are good news because they bring us face to face with God in Christ as savior, redeemer, sanctifier, forgiver, mediator, reconciler, source of all life and source of all love.

The Christian life is a continual conversion, a continual turning again and again to God as author and sustainer of all life. The goal of this conversion process is to experience ever afresh our graced and intimate relationship with God and our relatedness to one another in Christ. In the process "the people of God become in this world a sign of conversion to God" (General Introduction, *Rite of Penance*, no. 4). The converted themselves become important signs to others about what life is all about, signs that our destiny lies in God alone.

Repentance and conversion, when based on God's Word, are indeed "good" news requiring effective proclamation in our words and actions. The process of conversion ought to make us joyful and serene, not dismal and glum. As a lifelong process, it does not require that we condemn the world or despair of our place in it; rather, repentance and conversion require that we put ourselves and our world in proper perspective.

What follows is divided into two parts. The first deals with the classical triad of fasting, prayer, and almsgiving as signs of conversion and Church renewal. The second deals with the place that the Word of God has in repentance and conversion. Examples will be drawn from the liturgy of the season of Lent, the prime time for repentance and deep conversion. My thesis is that the ascetical practices of fasting, prayer, and almsgiving, as well as prayerful reflection on and proclamation of the Word, constitute essential aspects of the Christian life. We will be concerned with the meaning of these practices, not just their historical precedent and traditional character, because, to use the words of the poet, in using them "we [may] have had the experience but missed the meaning."[2]

Liturgy and sacraments take place in the context of human life and of the journey of Christian faith. They validate Christian identity in the world and mark important stages in life's journey to the Kingdom. Ascetical practices help provide the context in which the liturgy of forgiveness and penance should take place. It is necessary, therefore, to examine the meaning inherent in ascetical practices so that we can understand them as key experiences in our journey to God.

1. ASCETICAL PRACTICES

Ten years ago Aidan Kavanagh wrote a powerful essay entitled "Christian Initiation: Tactics and Strategy."[3] He observed that the clearest symptom of the present state of the church was the quality of recent discussion on Christian initiation. He stated that far too many of the issues surrounding initiation concerned tactical matters only, for example, the age for confirmation and first Communion, or how to deal with parents presenting their children for baptism. Such issues, he said, were tactical and strategic only; they did not hit at the real value and meaning of Christian initiation—lifetime conversion to the gospel.[4]

We need to revive this important distinction between tactics and vision as we examine the Church's traditional ascetical practices of fasting, prayer, and almsgiving. These practices have been understood by the Church to be essential means, not ends, to signify conversion to the gospel. Fasting has enjoyed a certain revival in recent spiritual writing[5] and contemporary pastoral practice, with explanations that we need to fast in order to demonstrate in our bodies what we believe in our minds and hearts.

The Roman Catholic tradition of liturgy and asceticism has always striven to uphold the bodiliness of the Christian life. The flesh is the instrument of salvation, said Tertullian.[6] It is through our actions and in our bodies that we demonstrate our belief in and conversion to God. This is not a matter for souls, ideas, or wills only; it is so central that it has to be reflected in the way we live our daily lives. Hence the usefulness of the theological tag "faith and morals." The one necessarily affects the other; together they reflect the converted Christian, or at least the Christian engaged in the deepening process of conversion. For enfleshed human beings, fasting makes sense. The vision that the tactics of fasting discloses is nothing other than a radical conversion to the ways of God.

However, fasting can also be (mis)understood as strategic or tactical only. We lose the vision of conversion when we try to explain fasting in utilitarian terms and emphasize the money to be saved from our fasting, money to help feed those who do not have enough to eat. This pragmatic line of reasoning offers only a typical approach. In the spiritual tradition of the Church, ascetical practices are meant to reflect the vision of what the Christian life is about. They are important only to the extent that they signify the deeper reality of conversion to God's ways and to God's will above all other wills and ways, especially our own. If they do not signify or demonstrate this conversion, they can easily be reduced to pragmatic or utilitarian usages. Anthony Bloom states that the whole aim and purpose of asceticism is "to become open."[7] The main purpose of fasting is that we become open to God and to the continual call of the gospel—in short, open to conversion.

The radicalness of this kind of conversion is evident over against the prevailing values of our world, where having, consuming, investing, and producing are rampant. We simply do not believe that "less is more"; rather, we seem to believe that "much" is not enough. Diametrically opposed to this is the ethos of the gospel that dispossession is better than possessing and that searching for God is better than searching for what profits here and now.

Robert Taft has argued that there is a prevailing spiritual ideology today that has been prevalent for the past thirty years. This spirituality "tells us that since God became man Christ is in our neighbor, and the real work of Christian spirituality is not to leave the world but to dive in and grab life with both hands. Justice is more important than mortification, love more important than celibacy . . . ."[8] He then goes on to say:

> One result of this contemporary spiritual ideology is that it has dealt a death blow to fasting, penance, mortification. Today among contemporary religious one hears more of gourmet cooking than of fasting—a striking countersymbol to anyone even superficially acquainted with the spiritual literature at the origins of religious life.[9]

These are piercing words. They may make us uncomfortable. Yet I use them here to indicate the situation we may well find ourselves in when we try to speak about asceticism and how it relates to forgiveness and reconciliation. There are at least two factors that Taft raises implicitly here that need to be addressed as we determine the place of asceticism in our lives. The first concerns the legalism and pragmatism often associated with asceticism. The second concerns how we understand the Christian's place in the world.

a) *Legalism and Pragmatism*

At the very time when we have experienced the shift in spirituality that Taft calls a "spiritual ideology" of misguided incarnationalism, we Catholics have also experienced a great freedom from legalistic prescriptions with regard to fasting and ascetical practices. This legalism was a most unfortunate carry-over from the preconciliar era. It is significant that more traditional expositions of fasting, for example from the Rule of St. Benedict, prescribed fasting with the most delicate phrasing and without severity. While the monk is to "love fasting" (RB 4:13),[10] Benedict was most reluctant to prescribe exact amounts of food or drink.[11] Even though Benedict himself cites others who maintain that monks should not drink wine at all, with characteristic understanding he states, "but since the monks of our day cannot be convinced of this, let us at least agree to drink moderately, and not to the point of excess" (RB 40:6).

Benedict states that the life of the monk should be "a continuous Lent" (RB 49:1). But then he immediately adds that "since few, however, have the strength for this, we urge the entire community during these days of Lent to keep its manner of life most pure and to wash away . . . the negligences of other times" (RB 49:2-3). The monks are to do this by additional "private prayer and abstinence from food and drink" (RB 49:5). These ascetical practices are profitable only if they are undertaken for the sake of conversion. Any such ascetical act is undertaken with the knowledge of the abbot, lest it be "reckoned as presumption and vain glory, not deserving a reward" (RB 49:9).

Finally, Benedict states that the superior may break his fast "for the sake of a guest" (RB 53:10), except on solemn fast days, since showing hospitality is a more important virtue than the external observance of fasting. Above all, fasting should not be a cause for grumbling in the community (RB 40:8). When undertaken in this spirit, fasting plays a key role in controlling passions. This control results in serenity, refinement, detachment, freedom, and joy; thus, it can be described as "really a source of joy."[12]

Fasting is a means to an end. The ascetical tradition of Christianity holds that fasting is primarily a sign of complete surrender and conversion to God, and that it is therefore tied to prayer and almsgiving. It is a sign of the kind of surrender to God exemplified in the obedience of Sarah and Abraham to God's incredible promise that they would have a son and numerous offspring (Gen 15–22; Rom 4). It is the kind of surrender exemplified by Mary's *fiat* and obedient service to God's message that she would bear the Son of the Most High (Luke 1:26-38). It is the kind of complete surrender to God that characterized Jesus' voluntary surrender of his life that we might be redeemed—"a death he freely accepted."[13] It is the kind of surrender that is poignantly described in the poet's phrase "Quick now, here, now, always—A condition of complete simplicity/(Costing nothing less than everything)."[14] The price of complete surrender is high, but the stakes are high too. What is the Christian life if not life lived on God's terms? Acceptance of these terms brings true and abiding Christian joy.

Now, it is clear that almsgiving is part of the triad and that charity is an essential Christian virtue. But this is to move too quickly. The crucial hinge between fasting and almsgiving is prayer, as St. Benedict noted. Prayer prevents fasting from becoming self-discipline or a program of asceticism that shows what we can do for God. Prayer prevents fasting and almsgiving from becoming marks of pride in what we can do to gain salvation. The spiritual life is really the other way around. It is God who inspires, supports, and sustains all that we do by our works of asceticism. Fasting, prayer, and the giving of alms are signs of surrender to God, but it is God who inspires us to undertake them in the first place. The opening prayer on the Thursday after Ash Wednesday is a stark reminder that God inspires all our ascetical acts, especially in Lent. We pray:

> Direct, O Lord, all our actions by your holy inspiration and carry them on by your gracious assistance so that our every prayer and work may begin in you and through you be brought to perfection.[15]

Prayer as openness to God in listening, dialogue, and surrender is the crucial hinge between fasting and giving alms. Fasting and alsmgiving are correlative, not because saving money usually used for food enables us to provide for the poor, but because they are signs of surrender to God. We fast to show our total dependence on God and to signify our desire to do without anything that might entice us to be self-satisfied or sated without God. We give alms as part of this same surrender. Almsgiving demonstrates another level of being free from the things of this world. It is not primarily an act of charity, which in itself could lead to exalting oneself and to pride. Prayer checks our pride, the greatest obstacle to conversion to God. [16]

b) *Christian Self-understanding*

A second issue about fasting concerns the Christian's place in the world and how the Christian views the world. If Catholic piety before the Second Vatican Council could be described as overly eschatological, if its symptoms were disdain for and condemnation of the world, and if its by-products were a negative outlook on the world, then the shift to incarnationalism is all to the good. An incarnational spirituality restores a balance and redirects attention to the fact that we live and work in a world that has not been condemned; it is this same world that God sent his Son to redeem. This world is the only one we know; it is this world that God loved and loves still.

Yet, incarnationalism need not mean complacency with the way things are or that asceticism no longer has a place. In fact, it is precisely the example of the incarnate Jesus that leads us to re-examine the relative merits of fasting as well as feasting. Jesus' own fasting in the wilderness was an expression of complete surrender to and trust in the Father (Matt 4:1-2 and par.).

> [Jesus'] sojourn in the desert and his fast is a kind of replica of humanity's long preparation for the coming of the Messiah and the inauguration of the Kingdom. Fast is related to the time of waiting. After the public ministry has begun,

he can say with good reason that the Kingdom is already
here. The Bridegroom has come, and it is not fitting that
the friends of the Bridegroom fast while he is with them;
in the time of accomplishment fast has no more meaning.
Once Christ is risen, fasting will only be appropriate in so
far as it marks the road of faith, the dimension of preparation and construction in the Christian life. [17]

We believe that the world is sacred because of Christ's
incarnation among us. The fact of Jesus' taking on human
flesh, living our life, dying our death, and rising to new
life demonstrates the uniqueness and special character of
the Christian faith. We also believe that Christ is to come
again. In fact, we Christians believe that we live between
the times of redemption accomplished and redemption
completed, of salvation won once for all in time and the
return of the Lord at the end of time to bring time to an
end. There is an eschatological edge and demand to our
faith. We forget or ignore this at our peril. This eschatological demand requires ascetical practices so that we can
be converted more and more fully in this imperfect world
to the Lord who came to set us free. We live between the
incarnation and the *eschaton* as the pilgrim Church. We
display our pilgrim status by the way we live life. As the
second Lenten preface states,

> You teach us how to live in this passing world with our heart
> set on the world that will never end.

We live now as Church; as the Church we yearn for the
Kingdom.

> [T]he ecclesial significance of fasting must be insisted upon.
> The Church on earth is awaiting its fulfillment and, at the
> same time, it is already in possession of it. Day after day [the

Church] advances toward the kingdom, [yet] she also manifests it already. [18]

To engage in fasting, prayer, and almsgiving is to demonstrate our pilgrim status. We have here no lasting city. The ascetical practices of fasting, praying, and giving alms become all the more essential in our age when the here and now appears to be all that there is. They are crucial acts of witness in a culture that distrusts the past, exalts the present, and regards the future as more of the present. For the Christian to engage in ascetical practices is to recall the past of saving history, especially the sojourn of Israel and Jesus in the desert, and by fasting in the desert to put life in proper perspective. To quote Taft again,

> . . . it was not to flee the world that God led his people, John the Baptist, Jesus and later the anchorites and hermits into the desert, but rather that they might manifest there, where the battle is most difficult, his victory and his rights. If Christ retired to the desert after his miracles, it was not to escape but to encounter the power of God. [19]

Every year in Lent we retire to the desert, but not to shun or condemn the world—that is anti-evangelical and anti-Christian. We retire to the desert as Christ did on the first Sunday of Lent to elect catechumens and to join them in their final weeks of battle toward our common goal of Christian conversion.

It is appropriate that on Ash Wednesday every year we hear the words of Matthew's Gospel (6:1-6, 16-18) and learn again the kind of fasting, prayer, and almsgiving that God wants—not for show, done in secret, and above all in humility. The Office of Readings on Ash Wednesday and the first reading at the Eucharist on the following Friday and Saturday repeat Isaiah's penetrating challenge that our fasting be pure lest it end in quarreling or jealousy (Isa 58).

Salvation history began in a garden and was

vitiated by food; the Good News opens in the desert and is accompanied by fasting. This is the antinomy of salvation history posed symbolically by Lent. Only by prayer and fasting are some devils cast out (Mk 9:29). Hence the desert is the perfect type of the "world" in the New Testament sense. It is the kingdom of Satan, hostile to God. It is there that the Son of Man must preach the Good News. The "desert theme" of Lent, therefore, is not an invitation to flee the real world . . . . The world of the Christian standing in vigil before God is just as "real" as any "real," and those who have never experienced it are the ones stuck in an irrelevant and unreal ghetto. [20]

To fast is also to summon the future when there will be no more fasting or ferias but only the eschatological banquet of the Kingdom for which we longed while on earth (Rev 19:5-9). The validity of fasting is judged by "its ability to foster union with Christ in faith, hope and love, and by its capacity to prepare us for eternal life." [21] Fasting, prayer, and almsgiving here and now are essential means of dealing with temptation and sin in the deserts of our hearts, and of making us mindful that this world leads to new heavens and a new earth, to a world that will never end. Ascetical practices, especially in Lent, orient us toward our future in God. [22] We celebrate sacraments and engage in ascetical practices so that we can become real and effective signs of conversion while living here and now in our imperfect world. Is it any wonder that Jesus, after his baptism and temptation, begins his ministry with the words "Reform your lives! The kingdom of heaven is at hand!" (Matt 3:17)?

2. REFLECTIVE READING AND PROCLAMATION OF THE WORD

The Introduction to the *Rite of Penance* states that the Church accomplishes and perfects continual repentance in different ways, among which are penitential services, the proclamation of the Word of God, prayer, and the penitential parts of the Eucharistic celebration (no. 4). I have already pointed out the essential role that prayer plays in ascetical practices of conversion. Here I want to argue that prayerful reflection on and proclamation of the Word of God is another essential means of fostering conversion and repentance. It does this in three movements: purgation, formation, and transformation. It is the Word that makes conversion a joyful process.

a) *Purgation*

The proclamation of the Word at the liturgy may well be interpreted, among other things, as an act of purgation drawing its hearers to repentance, conversion, and union with God. For example, exegetes parallel Matthew's inclusion of the text "for the forgiveness of sins" at the Last Supper (Matt 26:28) with Jesus' healing statement to the paralytic, "Have courage, son, your sins are forgiven" (Matt 9:2). Significantly, the text about the forgiveness of sins at the Last Supper has remained to this day in the Eucharistic Prayer. The word spoken to the paralytic is deliberately phrased to demonstrate that Jesus' power goes beyond physical healing; more to the point of this healing is the revelation that "the Son of Man has authority on earth to forgive sins" (Matt 9:6).[23]

This understanding of the power of Jesus' word goes back to creation in Genesis 1 and to the hymn about the incarnate Word in John 1. These scriptural images of the power of God's Word must be understood whenever we hear the word proclaimed at the liturgy, especially the Eucharist. This is to suggest that the Liturgy of the Word is always an act of creation. It is an act whereby God's words are spoken not for information or for theological reflection or even for instruction (too often reduced to moralizing) about how to act in life; they are proclaimed first and foremost to create us again in God's image and likeness. The first moment of that process is an act of purgation.

The Word challenges, exhorts, and chides us. It lays bare our defects and defenses. It is God's way of inviting us into divine life. The price is to lay aside evil and sinful ways. The Word thus proclaimed is rightly accompanied by the rubric "May the words of the gospel wipe away our sins."[24] Just as John the Baptist acclaims the Word incarnate as the Lamb of God who takes away our sins (John 1:29), so do we acclaim the "Lord Jesus Christ" in praise and thanks for the Word we hear at the liturgy.

No clearer description of the process of purgation which the Word is sent to accomplish can be found than that in John 15 about the vine and the branches. Jesus states that he is the true vine, as opposed to the unfaithful and unfruitful vine often imaged in the Old Testament.[25] His followers are grafted onto him through the Word he proclaims. Real life for believers is God's life; this life comes from hearing and obeying the Word. Only if we live in the incarnate Word and his words stay part of us (John 15:7) can we have any hope that what we ask will be heard by the Father. The vine analogy explicitates what was hinted at in the healing of the paralytic—that it is continual hearing of and submission to the Word that makes us true disciples.

This requires that we who make up liturgical communities open our hearts, not just our minds, to hearing the Word. We have to allow the probing and searching nature of God's Word to penetrate well-worn habits that are less than virtuous so that we can be among the fruitful, truly living members of the vine. This process is what classical treatises call "holy reading,"[26] the chief aim of which is union with God through conformity to the Word. This exercise is not primarily of the mind but of the will and heart.[27] To change one's mind is relatively easy compared with changing one's life.

At sacramental celebrations the restoration of the Word has a deep theological significance. We who are formed again and again through the Word as God's chosen ones move from the proclaimed Word to the enacted Word of sacraments to be strengthened by the sacred rites thus celebrated. But it is always the Word that creates us anew, because it purges us of our sin and invites us into a life that is ever new in the incarnate Word.

The Fathers of the Church use many expressions to describe this process:

> . . . the Word of God *touches* our heart, it *wounds*, it *needles*, it *pierces*, it *cleaves* our heart *open*. The Word *jolts* our heart *awake*. "Wake up, sleeper" (Eph 5:14). At the very centre of a man, at his core, in his heart, the new light arises. It is the same God that said, "Let there be light shining out of darkness," and who has shone in our minds (hearts) to radiate the light of the knowledge of God's glory, the glory on the face of Christ" (2 Cor 4:6).[28]

Purgation is the first moment in the process of being made new and a member of God's true vine.

b) *Formation*

The second moment in listening to the Word occurs both in individual reflection on the Word and in its liturgical proclamation—it transforms us and our comprehension of who God is and what life in union with God really means. There is a divine logic in the Word, but it is a logic that defies human judgment and expectation. Most often this divine logic is disclosed in parables, especially those that shock us or go against our sense of "fair play."

> Symbols and symbolic narratives express [one's] consciousness of . . . sin, as well as . . . [one's] hope for redemption. Related to parables in the living context of New Testament proclamation and community celebration, they challenge [our] conscience, by questioning the very ground of [our] existence and the horizons within which [we live].[29]

Take the example of the parable of the laborers sent into the vineyard (Matt 20:1-16). Our sense of fair play, not to mention retributive justice, is set back by this story of God's treating the last like the first. God's mercy knows no limits. While we would freely admit this as a principle of our biblical knowledge of God, it does rub us the wrong way when we think that public sinners and "come lately" types will enter the same kingdom we will enter, that is, if we will have remained faithful to the end. Is that not the point of the Matthean images of weeds and wheat (Matt 13:24-30)? In our zeal, are we not sometimes like the workers who want to pull up the weeds at their first appearance lest they drain (or overshadow) the wheat? The landowner's reply is at first curious, "Let them grow together until harvest" (v. 30). But the reply becomes less and less curious when we realize a deeper level of meaning here, namely, that the Church is composed of both weeds and wheat and that it is only at the end that a final judgment can be made as to which is which or who is who. The poignancy here is that some who think they are wheat may well be weeds, and some who start out as weeds may well be wheat at the final judgment. The message is clear: Leave both until harvest, and leave the judgment to God alone.

Or what about the Lukan parable about hospitality at a large dinner (Luke 14:16-24)? Those who were initially invited do not show up, so the outcasts of society become the honored guests. The poor, the maimed, the blind, the lame become those who are treated to special hospitality in the Kingdom. The parable is all the more poignant when we consider that none of us is worthy of the Kingdom. Each one of us must acknowledge that we are the poor, the maimed, the blind, and the lame who will be exalted only if and when we acknowledge our need for God and for the Kingdom.

Finally, what about the most poignant of symbolic narratives—the parables of the lost sheep, the lost coin, and the prodigal son (Luke 15)? The setting itself discloses a startled cadre of religionists, the scribes and Pharisees, who take issue with Jesus for eating at table with sinners. The first two parables reveal a way of acting that overturns accepted human expectations. One lost sheep or silver coin is relatively insignificant compared to the ninety-nine sheep or nine coins still safe. To search for a sheep and risk the loss of the herd, or to search for a coin and lose a day's pay (plus money for the party to celebrate the found coin) is certainly bad economics, but it is good Christianity. It is a fine image of the Christian God revealed in Jesus. Who of us does not rely on this parable when we find ourselves among the lost, the wayward, and the marginal?

To ponder the Word requires that we allow it to form our notions about who God is and what Christianity is all about. It is not retributive justice, an eye for an eye, or facile judgments about virtue and vice. It is about how we open ourselves to God and allow God to form us again and again into the divine image and likeness. The formative power of the Word is crucial in order that God's ways of dealing with us become habits of the heart and habitual ways of dealing with one another. Such a process obviously involves repentance and conversion again and again so that we can live the values of the Kingdom, as demanding as they are.

c) *Transformation*

The final function of the Word is transformation. This occurs in the liturgical proclamation of the Word because it is here that God's direct address reaches us directly and personally. I argued above that fasting is an eschatological action in that it is a sign of the Kingdom to come. I want to parallel that statement by stating that the Liturgy of the Word is an eschatological experience. In the Liturgy of the Word we experience far more than thoughts about God or instructions about the Kingdom. It is in and through liturgy that we experience anew the meaning of symbols, symbolic narratives, and parables. What happened *in illo tempore* ("at that time") happens to us still "in this time," in our day and age, in the liturgy. The characters of the parables are ourselves. The life settings of parables are the setting of our lives. The actions of God

to give resolution and insight, forgiveness and invitation
to life are repeated for us in the liturgy not primarily for
our instruction but for our transformation. The Liturgy
of the Word is about address, response, hearing, pondering, and understanding. But it is primarily an experience
of the Kingdom of God active among us.

It is signficant, I think, that on the second Sunday of
Lent we are invited beyond the temptation and fasting of
Jesus to share in his transfiguration. It is in that most significant of salvation-history settings, a mountain, that
Christ is revealed in all his glory. It is from heaven that
God's voice is heard (as it was at his baptism and as it will
be at his crucifixion) identifying Jesus as God's Son with
the command "Listen to him" (Matt 17:5; Mark 9:7; Luke
9:35). The transfiguration account fittingly follows the
temptation at which Jesus says that we live not on bread
alone but on every word that comes from the mouth of
God (Matt 4:4). [30] The scene of Christ's transfiguration continues this motif and invites us to experience our own transfiguration into people of the Kingdom through the
proclaimed and preached Word of God. And yet the
prayers for this Sunday are carefully crafted to disclose that
while we experience Christ's glory at the liturgy, we also
long for its fullness in the Kingdom:

> Almighty God,
> who have commanded us to hear the Word of your beloved
>   Son,
> grant that we may be nourished and purified by that Word,
> and, in the age to come, be made joyful
> by the vision of your glory.
>
> *(opening prayer)*

Heavenly Father,
we thank you for having given us, while yet on earth,
a foretaste of the joys of heaven
in the holy sacrament we have received.[31]

(prayer after Communion)

Not surprisingly, for the Word to take deep root in our hearts as constitutive of repentance and conversion, it is necessary that we be prepared for the kind of lifelong but necessary conflict described by Gregory the Great:

> The place of battle is the heart of the one who hears the word of God. It is called a place of battle because there the word which is received makes war on well-worn ways of life . . . . What does it mean, then, to come to the place of battle if not by the approach of acute discernment, to come to the very depths of the heart of the listener, where the enemies may most quickly be found and most ruthlessly cut to pieces? For those who do not know how to wage an internal conflict can never come to the true battlefield.[32]

It was noted above that conversion and repentance were required because in the Matthean text Jesus proclaims the presence and urgency of the Kingdom. It is significant that this text is an adjustment from the Markan account, now used as the second formula for imposing ashes on Ash Wednesday, "Repent and believe the gospel" (Mark 1:15).[33] We repent during Lent to be converted to the gospel, which, when proclaimed liturgically, is itself an experience of the Kingdom whose coming we long for and whose values we seek to live here and now.

What I have argued here concerns fundamental Christian attitudes about life and faith and what Christianity is all about. Seen from the perspective of the joy that comes to those who share in God's Kingdom, conversion and repentance themselves are joyful, since they lead us to knowledge of our real selves and to experience God's forgiveness of our faults and failures. Yet it is essential to recall that this whole process is God-inspired, God-directed, and God-destined. In the words of St. Bernard,

> If a great good is not to be twisted into a great evil, it is of paramount importance for every one among you who seek God to understand that he anticipates you, and that you are being sought before you sought him. The soul seeks the word, but it was first sought by the Word. [34]

When all is said and done, conversion and repentance are demands of God's Kingdom so that we can enter that Kingdom worthily and fully as God's sons and daughters. We have seen that acts of asceticism and pondering and proclaiming the Word of God are fundamentally eschatological experiences. But these are already experienced here and now in the Church's liturgy, especially in Lent and Easter. The texts of Lent put this into perspective. They continually remind us that conversion and repentance in Lent are not for Easter day or the Easter season. They are what all liturgy is for—the experience of the fullness of the Kingdom forever. In the words of the preface for the First Sunday of Lent,

> His fast of forty days
> makes this a holy season of self-denial.
> By rejecting the devil's temptations
> he has taught us
> to rid ourselves of the hidden corruption of evil,
> and so to share his paschal meal in purity of heart,
> until we come to its fulfillment
> in the promised land of heaven.

Sometimes we Catholics, even the more initiation-conscious of us, tend not to look toward Lent as a high point. More often than not, we probably would like to say what Groucho Marx said to the priest on that street in Montreal—it takes the joy out of life. But it is then that we should recall the eschatological nature of the season, of Easter, and of our whole lives. Lent is a privileged time for putting life into perspective and to realize again that what matters is what this life leads to—a new heavens and a new earth. What we experience here and now "in a glass darkly"—God's very life and love—will be revealed fully and finally. We shall never again hunger or thirst or mourn or fear, because the God whom we knew on earth and for whom we longed will draw us near once for all.

> Never again shall they know hunger or thirst,
>   nor shall the sun or its heat beat down on them,
>   for the Lamb on the throne will shepherd them.
> He will lead them to springs of life-giving water,
>   and God will wipe every tear from their eyes.
>   (Rev 7:16-17)

Hence the importance of the familiar hymn text we sing in Lent to accompany our annual Lenten journey with fast, prayer, almsgiving, and prayerful reflection on the Word of God:

> Abide with us, that so, this life
> Of suff'ring over past,
> An Easter of unending joy
> We may attain at last!

NOTES

1. John Shea, *The Challenge of Jesus* (New York: Doubleday Image Books, 1977) 72.

2. T.S. Eliot, "The Dry Salvages," *The Four Quartets*, in *The Complete Poems and Plays* (New York: Harcourt, Brace and Co., 1952) 133.

3. Aidan Kavanagh, in *Made, Not Born: New Perspectives on Christian Initiation and the Catechumenate* (Notre Dame: University of Notre Dame Press, 1976) 1–6.

4. *Ibid.* 1–2.

5. For example, Joseph F. Wimmer, *Fasting in the New Testament: A Study in Biblical Theology* (New York: Paulist Press, 1982); John A. Gurrieri, "Fasting: A Tradition Rediscovered," *Liturgy: Feasts and Fasting* (Washington: The Liturgical Conference, 1981) 59–64; Irene Nowell, "Food Is God's Gift," *ibid.* 9–13.

6. See Cipriano Vagaggini, *Caro Salutis Est Cardo* (Rome: Desclee, 1966).

7. Anthony Bloom, quoted in Aidan Kavanagh, "Liturgy and Ecclesial Consciousness: A Dialectic of Change," *Studia Liturgica* 15 (1982–83) 20.

8. Robert Taft, "Lent: A Meditation," *Beyond East and West: Problems in Liturgical Understanding* (Washington: Pastoral Press, 1984) 49.

9. *Ibid.*

10. All translations from the Rule of St. Benedict are from Timothy Fry, ed., *RB 1980: The Rule of St. Benedict in Latin and English with Notes* (Collegeville: The Liturgical Press, 1981).

11. For a thorough commentary on fasting in the Rule of St. Benedict (particularly during Lent) as compared with the Rule of the Master and other sources, see Adalbert DeVogüé, *La Règle de saint Benoît: Commentaire historique et critique*, vol. 6 (Paris: Les Éditions du Cerf, 1971) 1205–34. For a spiritual reflection on the contemporary practice of fasting, see DeVogüé, "To Love Fasting: An Observance That Is Possible and Necessary Today," *American Benedictine Review* 35 (Sept. 1984) 302–13. For an overview of fasting in the patristic era, see Herbert Musurillo, "The Probelm of Ascetical Fasting in the Greek Patristic Writers," *Traditio* 12 (1956) 1–64.

12. DeVogüé, "To Love Fasting" 309.

13. The original in Hippolytus' anaphora states: "(7) Fulfilling your will and gaining for you a holy people, he stretched out his hands when he should suffer, that he might release from suffering those who have

believed in you. (8) And when he was betrayed to voluntary suffering that he might destroy death, and break the bonds of the devil, and tread down hell, and shine upon the righteous, and fix the limit, and manifest the resurrection . . . ." In R.C.D. Jasper and G.J. Cuming, *Prayers of the Eucharist, Early and Reformed* (London: Collins, 1975) 22.

14. T.S. Eliot, "Little Gidding," *The Four Quartets* 145.

15. Since the Latin original of this collect is not adequately reflected in the translation in the Sacramentary, the translation provided is my own. There is a certain tongue-in-cheek quality to the use of this text on the day after Ash Wednesday. "Well begun" is not "half done" in Lent, in the sense that the Christian must strive to persevere through the rest of the season. Hence the inspirational quality of this prayer.

16. André Louf puts the matter directly in his essay "Repentance and Experience of God," *Monastic Studies* 9 (1972) 23–39, at 29: "Obedience, asceticism, even prayer can be directed away from the living God and made to serve an ideal of perfection not differing essentially from a secular ethic. They then become works of man and his stronghold, a rampart he erects against others and sometimes against God. In such a 'system of justice,' repentance, if it remains at all, becomes a single exercise alongside others. But it is no longer the miracle of grace that entirely transforms man, the threshold across which he begins to be born into a new existence—making him completely free in the desires of the Holy Spirit."

17. Thierry Maertens and Jean Frisque, *Guide for the Christian Assembly*, vol. 3, trans. Molaise Meehan, O.S.B. (Notre Dame, Ind.: Fides Publishers, 1971) 138–39.

18. *Ibid.* 55.

19. R. Taft, "Lent" 54.

20. *Ibid.*

21. J. Wimmer, *Fasting in the New Testament* 124.

22. See Thomas J. Talley *Origins of the Liturgical Year* (New York: Pueblo Publishing Co., 1986) on the association of Lent with the fast of Jesus (pp. 189–94) and the relationship between Lent and penitence (pp. 222–25). He concludes the latter by saying: "In the face of that promise [complete redemption through Jesus' death and resurrection] those reaching toward faith in the initiatory process, those lost to the community seeking reconciliation, and all who have learned in faith that both new birth and reconciliation are but sacraments pointing *to realities that rush toward us from the future,* all alike know the time that moves toward Pascha as the time for metanoia, the time of con-

version, the time of repentance, the time that identifies our human lives and all our human history as the process of conversion moving now and always to meet the coming of the Lord at the consummation of the age" (pp. 224–25, emphasis mine).

23. See, Georg Strecker, *Der Weg der Gerechtigkeit: Untersuchung zur Theologie des Matthäus* (Göttingen: Vandenhoeck und Ruprecht, 1971) 220–22.

24. See Joseph Jungmann, *The Mass of the Roman Rite*, vol. 1, trans. Francis Brunner (New York: Benziger Brothers, 1950) 450–55. See also John Quinn, "The Lord's Supper and Forgiveness of Sin," in Kevin Seasoltz, ed., *Living Bread, Saving Cup* (Collegeville: The Liturgical Press, 1982) 241.

25. The vine imagery is exemplified in several texts, among which are Ps 80:16; Isa 5:1-7; Jer 2:21; Hos 10:1; Sir 24:17; Matt 21:23.

26. For an intriguing approach to this classical form of prayer, see Jean Leclercq, "Lectio Divina," *Worship* 58 (1984) 239–48.

27. See André Louf, *Teach Us to Pray: Learning a Little About God.* Trans. Hubert Hoskins (New York: Paulist Press, 1975).

28. *Ibid.* 38.

29. David N. Power, "The Sacramentalization of Penance," *The Heythrop Journal* 18 (1977) 16.

30. This text of Matt 4:4 (originally from Deut 8:3) is used as the gospel acclamation in all three Lectionary cycles on this Sunday.

31. These are my own translations.

32. Quoted in Aelred Squire, *Summer in the Seed* (New York: Paulist Press, 1979) 55–56.

33. The importance of "gospel" in the Markan narrative is noted by many exegetes, who point to its use here at the beginning (Mark 1:15), at the missionary command at its conclusion (Mark 16:15), and at several important places throughout the text. That it is clearly a part of Mark's editorial plan as opposed to the other synoptics is seen in the following: the conditions of discipleship in 8:35 (not found in the parallels in Matt 16:25 or Luke 9:24); in the story of the rich young man in 10:29 (not found in the parallels in Matt 19:29 or Luke 18:28b); and on the gospel being preached to the nations in 13:10 (not found in the parallels in Matt 24:18 or Luke 21:13).

34. Aelred Squire, *Asking the Fathers: The Art of Meditation and Prayer* (Wilton: Morehouse-Barlow, 1973) 32.

Reconciliation:
Disquieting Pastoral Reflections

KATHLEEN HUGHES, R.S.C.J.

My task is to explore pastoral concerns surrounding the revised rites of penance. Where have we been? Where are we today? What are our present needs and problems? In other words, what are the positive and negative signs of the times regarding the community's experience and celebration of reconciliation today?

This is a task that was urged on all professional liturgists by the National Conference of Catholic Bishops in their document *The Church at Prayer: A Holy Temple of the Lord*, which assessed liturgical renewal in the United States twenty years after the promulgation of the Constitution on the Sacred Liturgy. With regard to the sacrament of penance, the bishops noted:

> Although intensive study and discussion preceded formulation of the revised Rite of Penance, pastoral problems continue to surround the sacrament. The new rites of reconciliation emphasize the reality of both personal and social sin in the Christian community and affirm that Christians are reconciled with God through the ministry of the Church. The fact is, however, that the importance of this sacrament has declined in the lives of many Christians, who

are not likely to recover appreciation for it unless they are once again convinced of its role in their lives.[1]

In the last two days we have examined the Church as a healing, reconciling community and have explored the virtue of penance and the ways Christians do penance and are reconciled. Now ecclesiology and ascetical theology yield the floor to pastoral theology, or as some would call it, practical theology—a theology that takes as its point of departure contemporary events and the experience of contemporary men and women. Pastoral theology attempts to take the experience of the community seriously, because pastoral theologians are motivated by the presupposition that the Church is a dynamic reality and that its communal life and growth are continually subject to and conditioned by the ever-changing contemporary situation. A pastoral liturgical approach suggests that one can answer the question of *how* liturgy ought to be done only if one knows what Christians are like as contemporary people, how a compassionate God is invading their lives, how they experience rupture and reconciliation, whom they turn to for the ministry of forgiveness, and what liturgical rites might be strong enough to bear this experience and large enough to celebrate it.

I want to dwell for a moment longer on *experience* as the point of departure for theological reflection because I find the present situation in our Church so disquieting. I believe that there has been an extraordinary loss of pastoral leadership in the area of sacramental reconciliation for reasons we will explore later. Particularly disheartening in this regard is the apostolic exhortation *Reconciliation and Penance,* which was issued after the Synod on reconciliation (1983) and which bears little relationship to contemporary life-experience and concrete pastoral needs, particularly as articulated through Synod interventions by bishops from around the world.[2] The sheep and the shepherd do not seem to graze in the same pasture.

Ritual, discipline, and Church order are not ends in themselves but are meant to reflect and bring to expression the human religious experience of the community, rather than serve to absolutize one form or other of discipline and rite. In my opinion, we do not so much face a crisis of meaning regarding penance and reconciliation as an inability to recognize that the Spirit is as present in this age as ever, and is moving hearts in new ways that we must discover, for it is to these people that we minister.

Rahner captures well the reason why we must sustain a dialogue between tradition and human experience:

> Precisely because liturgiology has now become in actuality quite independent, practical theology as a whole will continually have the task of delivering liturgiology from the dangers of a romantic glorification of the old forms of the liturgy, the danger of an aesthetic view, of a rubricistic legalism and also of the private whim of the connoisseur. It will lead to a liturgy which can really be a liturgy of the People of God here and now.[3]

I develop the role of pastoral theology as a kind of apologia for what follows, specifically to underscore the fact that concern for what is happening in peoples' lives is not frivolous nor outside the ambit of *real* theology. Human experience is a necessary point of departure for serious theological reflection. So much for method.

I have reduced my reflections, disquieting and otherwise, to three main topics. First, I would like to deal with questions of frequency, form, location, and ministry with regard to sacramental reconciliation, strictly speaking, and in the process to suggest the *extraordinary* role of this sacrament in Christian life. Second, and as a direct corollary of the first, I would like to develop the *process* character of reconciliation. Third, I would like to address the *implementation* of the present sacramental rites under two rubrics: ignorance and retrenchment.

1. IS SACRAMENTAL RECONCILIATION ORDINARY OR EXTRAORDINARY?

Should sacramental reconciliation be an ordinary or an extraordinary event in the life of the Christian? This is a very important and fundamental question to explore, for the way we answer this question will dictate the answer to other questions of frequency, form, location, and ministry.

In his postsynodal apostolic exhortation of December 2, 1984, Pope John Paul II stated a series of convictions, the first of which was the following: "For a Christian, *the Sacrament of Penance is the ordinary way* of obtaining forgiveness and the remission of serious sins committed after Baptism."[4] Further in the same document we read: "The first form—*reconciliation of individual penitents*—is the only normal and ordinary way of celebrating the Sacrament, and it cannot and must not be allowed to fall into disuse or to be neglected."[5]

I would like to challenge these statements and to raise some cautions about two corollary positions as well, namely, that the Church is the ordinary place for reconciliation and that the priest is the ordinary minister. I challenge these assumptions because I view the sacrament of reconciliation, strictly speaking, as an *extraordinary* event in the life of a Christian which brings to culmination and public, ritual celebration a whole series of quite ordinary experiences of penance and reconciliation. Moreover, that the sacrament of penance, especially in its first form, is the ordinary means of obtaining forgiveness is not true of history or of theology, nor does it represent contemporary pastoral experience. To speak of it as if it did is to invite cognitive dissonance and the loss of credibility and leadership that naturally flow from perceived dissonance.

In the course of history Christian men and women have experienced sacramental reconciliation within the community in a great variety of ways. Perhaps no other sacrament has been as supple in adapting ritual expression to the felt needs of the times, often adopting new forms when older patterns of ritual activity had been abandoned, a fact in itself quite instructive for our present dilemma. The community has known sacramental celebrations both public and private, exceptional or widespread, simple or complex, harsh or lenient, juridical or medicinal, focused on the doing of penance, on the confession of sins, on one's relationship with God, on the holy life, on what the penitent does or on what the Church does. This has to convince us that it is impossible to state from a reading of history that the first rite, the Rite for Reconciliation of Individual Penitents, can be regarded as the ordinary way of celebrating the sacrament. History further instructs us that a sacrament only gradually evolved in the first several centuries of the Church, and then, in its infancy, this sacrament was a once-in-a-lifetime experience reserved for those guilty of grave, public sin—hardly your ordinary experience.

It follows that the community knew other, more ordinary means of reconciliation. From earliest times, if we are able to speak of any reconciling experience as "ordinary" in the life of Christians, we would have to name the Eucharist rather than penance as the ordinary means of reconciliation. As the Introduction to the *Rite of Penance* reminds us:

> In the sacrifice of the Mass the passion of Christ is made present; his body given for us and his blood shed for the forgiveness of sins are offered to God again by the Church for the salvation of the world. In the eucharist Christ is present and is offered as "the sacrifice which has made our peace" with God and in order that "we may be brought together in unity" by his Holy Spirit. [6]

It must be recognized, particularly in light of the virtue of penance and the role of prayer, fasting, and works of charity, that Christians have known a variety of ordinary means of reconciliation beyond those deemed strictly sacramental.

In this connection I stumbled on a further elaboration of ascetical practices when I was doing some research on the seven penitential psalms. It appears that these psalms, considered to form a class by themselves at least from the sixth century, had been interpreted allegorically to indicate the *seven* means of obtaining forgiveness as classically conceived: baptism, martyrdom, almsgiving, the possession of a forgiving spirit, conversion of a sinner, acts of love, and, finally, penance. [7]

History and theology are joined by contemporary experience in challenging the assertion that the sacrament of reconciliation, especially in its individual form of celebration, is under any circumstances "ordinary" today. Reports have stated this categorically. The importance of the sacrament has declined; participation in it has been drastically reduced. By what James Burtchaell called a kind of spooky simultaneity, Catholics simply discontinued the practice, perhaps at first postponing it longer than usual, and then, finding neither desire nor need, the postponement was extended into an indefinite wait. [8]

"Confession" as a reality and as a symbol was discovered to lack meaning, vitality, and function, and it simply ceased to operate in any real way in the lives of quite ordinary Christians. This happened, I think, prior to the promulgation of new rites—a chronology not without importance for the way the new rites were to be implemented, but that is to get ahead of ourselves.

Langdon Gilkey has made some interesting observations about once functioning social symbols which die not because one day we reject them, but which start to languish when our life-world recedes from them:

> It is clear that without touch with ordinary, shared experience, with the real life-world of day to day and so of today, symbols weaken in intrinsic power and validity, and lose their function and role. At first they become merely traditional, rote, even magical devices, extrinsic, heteronomous forms that crush rather than shape our true existence now rooted elsewhere. At last, however, all reality having fled to the new life-world, they are left inert and flat ghosts, emissaries of a lost world that is no longer real and embodying meanings that no longer mean. This slow bleeding to death of once omnipotent symbols is not totally strange to present Catholic experience. [9]

In light of the data of history, theology, and present pastoral experience, I think we must conclude that the meaning of the celebration of reconciliation of an individual penitent as "ordinary" is only true as a restatement of preconciliar discipline, observed today largely in the breach. But let me add immediately that we cannot, from this datum alone, make a judgment about the state of the Church, the lack of docility to the Church's magisterium, the loss of the sense of sin, the perversity of modern men and women, etc. The shift in ordinary Catholic sacramental practice must be regarded by pastoral theologians as neither good nor bad but neutral until interpreted in light of the social sciences and in dialogue with the Tradition.

A second question that I want to pose is this: Is the Church the ordinary place for reconciliation? This question is really twofold: Does reconciliation ordinarily happen in more formal Church structures, and the larger question, Is the Church perceived as a community of reconciliation? The former question we might answer very briefly. Ordinary reconciliation happens in quite ordinary places—over the breakfast table, in the car, over a drink. Reconciliation happens in the day to day where Christians live their lives. We will return to daily experiences of reconciliation when we develop reconciliation as process.

As for the larger question, Christians will recognize the Church as the ordinary place of reconciliation when our rhetoric corresponds with our reality. Some of you may have read about Cardinal Bernardin's televised mission during Holy Week a few years ago. I would wager that if any memory lingers among listeners, it is the Cardinal's opening words, which were a request for forgiveness for himself and other public ministers in the Church for ways in which they had not served well, had wounded the Body of the Church, had not been agents of reconciliation nor compassionate representatives of the healing Christ, who was himself beset by weakness and thus able to deal compassionately with others.

There is too little of this recognition of weakness and sinfulness on the part of the Church and its public ministers. The present climate within the Church puts the lie to this witness and reality. Archbishop John Roach's intervention at the Synod addressed the chronic rejection and alienation felt by some people within our community which they might easily ascribe to the Church or even to God. He named the rejection of those in the minority because of race, low income, psychological and physiological problems, minimal social skills, disordered family environments, and other factors that separate them from the mainstream. He could have added those separated because of gender, sexual orientation, divorce, remarriage, and theological stance. He said:

> Such people sometimes carry a diffused sense of guilt, stemming not from personal sin but from judgments rendered by the majority culture. Some cultures, for example, subtly regard personal prosperity and social success as signs of God's favor. The absence of such achievements can impose unrealistic burdens of guilt and a sense of divine rejection on numbers of people. Pastors must attempt to dispel such guilt and self-depreciation, for it is unrelated to personal sin. The pastor's acceptance of all penitents as sinners like himself is essential in reconciling the socially alienated Catholic. [10]

Archbishop Roach was one of numerous participants at the Synod who attempted to address the Church's necessary struggle against social and structural sin both within and without its walls, and the Church's responsibility to attempt reconciliation with those within the Church who for a variety of reasons experience the Church as the place not of reconciliation but of alienation. I developed this aspect of our topic at length at the University of Notre Dame in June under the rubric of our practice of "shunning," a practice analogous to the Amish practice of excommunication. I would not return to the topic now were it not for the exceptionally divisive climate of late in the American Church and the fact that shunnings and near shunnings are more and more prominent. What kind of witness do we give? How can we be, in truth, the locus of reconciliation under such circumstances? Does this not create another level of cognitive and affective dissonance?

My third question concerns the ordinary ministers of reconciliation in our lives. Just as reconciliation happens in most ordinary places, it also happens among most ordinary people. It happens between spouses, between parents and children, between friends. Reconciliation happens among soul friends as well, whether ordained or lay, men or women. We are all ambassadors of reconciliation, or so St. Paul tells us. But what if we take Paul's dictum seriously? What if we believe that all of us participate in this ministry? What then becomes of the role of the ordained minister in the mediation of God's forgiveness and peace?

A recent article by Rose Hoover raises that question, which she considers crucial in an age when many people seldom or never receive the sacrament of penance, and when more and more Catholics are turning to non-ordained men and women for spiritual counsel. She probes the question, explicitly recognizing that some in the community necessarily serve as official representatives of the Church in its ministry of reconciliation.

> For centuries, it has been the ordained priesthood which has represented the Church in the sacrament of penance. Integrity has been viewed as an open-hearted confession in the presence of the ordained minister of this sacrament. But what if the priest is not the one who, in a real way, represents

the Church for the penitent? In other words, what if the priest stands for the whole people of God in title only, while someone else is a more effective indication in this individual's life of that pentitential community which suffers with him, prays for him, proclaims forgiveness and in fact forgives him?[11]

Is confession sacramental under such circumstances? That, indeed, is a disquieting question for our reflection. Yet, if we are honest with ourselves, we can name just such experiences. I suspect most readers have known moments in their lives of genuine forgiveness and reconciliation, perhaps even brought to the point of "public, ritual celebration" through the mediation of another, a person who did not happen to be ordained to the ministry of reconciliation. Such events are outside "official" sacramental structures and ministries, in the ordinary time of our lives. And yet we know that they are profoundly sacramental.

In summary, members of the community experience reconciliation events that they know and name as sacramental, experiences that take place outside official structures and without designated ministers, while sacramental reconciliation is an infrequent occurrence in our collective experience; and often, though we have not dwelt on this, it is either an annual or semi-annual celebration in the context of a communal rather than an individual rite. Meanwhile, outside of Advent and Lent, prayer, fasting, works of mercy, and participation in the Eucharist are among the many ways that Christians obtain forgiveness and the remission of sins and ritualize reconciliation in their lives.

2. SACRAMENTAL PROCESS

Let us now move on to the second topic for reflection in light of the data we have just reviewed. How are we to view these contemporary experiences and events? Are they aberrations to be rooted out, or are they indicative perhaps of another model now emerging of Church and sacrament, and particularly the sacrament of reconciliation? What if we were to propose that the several rites of reconciliation available within the community might best serve as *extraordinary* ways of bringing a journey of conversion to public ritual expression? In other words, what if we were to take sacramental process seriously? How would this stretch our understanding and practice of reconciliation?

The Rite of Christian Initiation of Adults (RCIA) stands as a paradigm for the renewal of all sacramental practice. It would serve us well in light of the contemporary experience of reconciliation to reflect very briefly on the ways in which the RCIA might help to redefine reconciliation.

First, the RCIA takes human religious experience seriously and recognizes that God works in many and various ways, that each human heart is unique, that conversion takes time, and that, as stated in the rite, nothing can be determined *a priori*. That suggests that just as first faith and conversion take place in the midst of the community, nurtured by the community in a variety of ways, so too the development of the experience of God's love and forgiveness in face of my own infidelity and sinfulness also takes time and may be nurtured in a variety of ways by other members of the community.

Just as the RCIA invites the many ministries of the community—catechesis, spiritual guidance, sponsorship, hospitality, and so on—so too does our present human experience suggest to us that there are many ministers of reconciliation within the community, each with a different gift and playing a different role. The entire community has been entrusted with the Church's ministry, in a diversity of roles.

Just as when one is enrolled in the catechumenate one becomes a member of the household of the faith and it is recognized that the sacramental process actually begins, sometimes extending for several years and concluding officially not at the font on the night of the great Vigil but actually fifty days later, so too it is possible to speak of the whole journey of reconciliation as sacramental process, from the first recognition of sin and alienation through the many ways of nurturing and ritualizing my deepening sense of God who rescues me from this body of death. We know in our heart of hearts that what we sometimes experience is sacramental. This gives us a way to name it as such and to welcome such a supple understanding of sacramental process that all the ordinary events, the ascetical practices, the interventions of God's grace in the mediations of others, the participation in the Eucharist could be seen as part of the nurturing and prolongation of the sacrament of reconciliation.

Just as the RCIA comes to full ritual expression in the water bath, anointing and banquet, a most *extraordinary* event that gathers up, expresses, and deepens the faith experience of the individual and the community, so too the Rite of Reconciliation of an Individual Penitent or a Celebration of Communal Reconciliation is an exceptional and extraordinary way of bringing to public, ritual expression the inner conversion of heart that has been nurtured in and outside official Church structures by the whole of the community as a priestly people. Recognition of the journey that precedes the celebration of sacrament, strictly speaking, avoids a too narrow focus on the rite, and thus the ever present danger of a magical or routine approach to sacrament. [12]

It is a process understanding of sacrament that undergirds the emerging order of penitents. It is a process model of reconciliation that makes sense of various ascetical practices. It is a process model that urges us to shift away from a narrow sense of the sacrament of penance to the recovery of the Church's mission of reconciliation, and in this context to see the sacrament as a culmination of all of the ways we make the sign of reconciliation to one another. It is process, in fact, that has been lost in the course of our history—both the understanding of the seeking after the holy life as a process, as well as the doing of penance as process of putting on, once again or more deeply, the mind and heart of Christ.

If, as I believe, the Rite of Christian Initiation of Adults has redefined the whole sacramental economy, then that rite may serve us well by providing both the sacramental principles and the structural model for a rediscovery of the role and celebration of reconciliation in the community. It is to the celebration of reconciliation in today's Church that we now turn.

The present rites and their implementation

After these two more theoretical excursions, we are now going to become quite concrete. I have two convictions about the present implementation: first, that there is still an appalling ignorance about the revised rites of recon-

ciliation on the part of the community and its ordained
ministers, particularly regarding the rite for reconciliation
of individual penitents, the very rite we have been told
is "ordinary"; and second, there is every evidence that before we have even discovered what the revised rites are
all about, we are ready to "throw in the towel" and give
up on the renewal. I propose that we look at the implementation of the rites, therefore, under the rubrics of ignorance
and retrenchment.

Ignorance. About a year and a half ago I wanted to
celebrate reconciliation. When I said to the priest that I
had chosen a passage of Scripture to begin the rite, he said
he thought that was a lovely idea. I thought it was a lovely
idea too, but I also knew that it was part of the rite. In
any case, I persevered, read the Scripture, and then opened
up my heart about my experience of sin and God's mercy,
the call to a new way of life, the extraordinary peace I
experienced, knowing myself loved and forgiven. When
I was finished the priest put up one hand in a gesture of
blessing, and without a word of response, without even
the naming of a penance, he began the formula of absolution. That quite unnerved me, as I realized that we had
moved into the emergency rite. I said to myself, "Have I
lost an engine? Is my ship sinking?"

My name is legion. It is difficult to find a confessor who
has interiorized the structure, the theology, and the spirit
of the rites. On the other hand, to be fair, it must be said
that the vast majority of Roman Catholics are also con-
fused, not altogether sure that there is a revised rite at all,
since they were told at the outset not to worry, for "little
had changed." This pastoral strategy of implementation,
namely, to tell people that nothing really had changed,

was a most devastating strategy, since confession as we knew it had already died, and what people wanted and needed to hear was that *everything* had changed. Moreover, from my vantage point of training those studying for the priesthood, I don't see quick solutions. It is very difficult to make good confessors out of individuals who have little or no personal experience of the rite upon which to draw for their own ministry of reconciliation.

Consider also this exchange between a priest and his penitent in a big downtown parish: The penitent began a listing of sins and the priest stopped him, inviting him to begin by recalling God's love that brought him to this moment and then to pray for light. Almost immediately the penitent began again with his confession. The priest urged him to take his time, to let this be an experience of prayer and so on, whereupon he was interrupted. "Look, Father, I know the rites. I'm a bishop. Could we get on with this, please."

Implementation of the Rite of Reconciliation of an Individual Penitent has been extraordinarily poor in many instances; in others, it has been nonexistent. There is a decided disease with ritual, with personal prayer in the presence of another, with the mutual transparency that this rite demands. All this is to suggest that we are only at the very beginning of the implementation of the rites, a fact which probably should not surprise us and which we ought to recognize and accept in light of the enormous amount of change in the last few years and the fact that Penance came at the tail end of so many changes. People were weary and/or annoyed with the whole situation of liturgical upheaval. The good news of this rite was stifled before it was ever discovered.

Since the celebration of the second rite, namely, Communal Reconciliation with Individual Confession and Absolution, will be predicated in part upon one's understanding of the content and the quality of the exchange between priest and penitent as in the first rite, the implementation of the second rite suffers a fate similar to that of the first rite, with the exception that in its implementation no one was able to explain away the genuinely new elements by saying that nothing had really changed. And, to their great credit, our communities have recognized the role of a communal rite to ritualize the public and social dimensions of sin and reconciliation and to express our supernatural solidarity, knowing that the sin of one harms all, just as the holiness of one redounds to the benefit of all. One undeniable sign of the times is the growing appreciation for communal reconciliation, a quite remarkable and healthy development, particularly in light of American individualism.

Regarding the use of the third rite, namely, the Rite of Reconciliation of Several Penitents with General Confession and Absolution, its implementation has been impeded almost from the day of its publication. This fact helps us shift to questions of retrenchment, as we first examine the brouhaha about the use of the third rite and what this may have communicated to our communities. Psychologists or psychiatrists looking in on our Church might say that we are now engaged in the classic double bind. ("Mother, may I please go out tonight?" "Of course, darling. I don't mind staying home alone. Enjoy yourself.")

We were told in the Constitution on the Sacred Liturgy that communal celebration of the liturgy is to be preferred (no 27). We are offered in the *Ordo Paenitentiae* of 1973 one individual and two communal forms of the Rite of Penance. The fact that the rite with general confession and absolution is inserted in the ritual on an equal footing with the other two *ordines* suggests that it is intended for use, even though the *praenotanda* regard it as extraordinary. In general, the provision of a variety of forms of penance would appear to be a genuine response to the needs of the times, with each form having a distinct but complementary value. How is it possible in this light to advocate one form to the detriment of the others or to prefer one form exclusively?

Add to this the judgment of most liturgists that the second form of the rite, namely, the Rite for Reconciliation of Several Penitents with Individual Confession and Absolution, could easily become a distortion of forms one and three and should be avoided, and we have the classic ingredients of the double bind. The communal is to be preferred, but don't use form two because it is a poor liturgical compromise, and don't use form three except with grave need "lest it subvert the values of individual reconciliation."[13]

Pastoral theologians and liturgists need to interpret the Church to itself in these circumstances, pointing out the problems and the very real dangers of such inconsistencies. Psychiatrists will tell you that double binds tend to produce schizophrenic children.

Retrenchment comes in two sizes this fall. Next month [November 1986] at the annual meeting of the National Conference of Catholic Bishops there will be the discussion of a *varium* concerning the first rite and the possibility, especially for children, of simplifying the ritual and of specifying a single act of contrition that should be learned by heart. In the last few years when I hear "simplify" I translate it "eliminate some of the options," "strip down the rite to its bare bones," "take away some of the last vestiges of potential adaptation." Aren't we only at the beginning of the renewal? Have we had enough experience with these rites to make any adaptations, particularly adaptations that involve the suppression of options? Do we not already have an act of contrition in the Eucharist that is one standard act for the community? Would we want to return to "O my God, I am heartily sorry . . ." and eliminate the possibility of personal expression of sorrow and love? I was alarmed when I heard about this *varium.*

The other instance of potential retrenchment is a further restriction of the use of the third form of reconciliation. I am told by those who have seen the canonical directives that they would make the use of the third rite virtually nonexistent.

Ignorance about the basic content of the Rite of Penance coupled with these current efforts of retrenchment sadden me because I have regarded its reform as one of the best kept secrets in the Church. As the last of the major rites to be revised, it found both clergy and community weary of change. It is understandable, human nature being what it is, that this ritual reform was downplayed, that the theological presuppositions were not developed, that the variety of ritual forms was not exploited, in the best sense, to nourish the community's ritual patterns of penance and reconciliation.

But that was twelve years ago. Should we continue to let this sacrament erode through ignorance, poor implementation, a general climate of retrenchment, and a hankering after the alleged stability of preconciliar discipline, life, and thought?

Pastoral problems will continue to surround the Rite of Penance as long as we have: the romantic glorification of old forms of liturgy; attempts, only twelve years after publication of the Rite of Penance, to suppress some of its ritual options; the presence, at least in ritual books, of appealing communal ritual forms that cannot or will not be used; the urging of frequency of individual confession on a community for whom old forms are evacuated of meaning and new forms have never been introduced.

Above all, pastoral problems will continue to surround the Rite of Penance until contemporary human religious experience of sin and grace, the ordinary and day-to-day experiences of forgiveness and reconciliation, the mediation of many ministers, and the variety of ways of bringing to expression the journey we are on are seen as integral to, and radically continuous with, the Church's sacramental life.

For this we pray to the Lord.

NOTES

1. National Conference of Catholic Bishops, *The Church at Prayer: A Holy Temple of the Lord* (Washington: United States Catholic Conference, 1983), no. 27, p. 14.

2. A thorough discussion of the work of the Synod as well as an analysis of the postsynodal apostolic exhortations has been provided by James Dallen, "Church Authority and the Sacrament of Penance: The Synod of Bishops," *Worship* 58:3 (May, 1984), 194–214; "*Reconciliatio et Paenitentia:* The Postsynodal Apostolic Exhortation," *Worship* 59:2 (March, 1985), 98–116. See also *Penance and Reconciliation in the Mission of the Church* (Washington: United States Catholic Conference, 1984) for a selection of interventions during the Synod.

3. Karl Rahner, "Practical Theology Within the Totality of Theological Disciplines," *Theological Investigations 9* (New York: Seabury Press, 1968) 113.

4. John Paul II, *Reconciliation and Penance: Post-Synodal Apostolic Exhortation of John Paul II to the Bishops, Clergy and Faithful on Reconciliation and Penance in the Mission of the Church Today* (Washington: United States Catholic Conference, 1984), no. 31:I, p. 115.

5. *Ibid.* no. 32, p. 128.

6. *The Rite of Penance* (Washington: United States Catholic Conference, 1975), no. 2.

7. R.E. Murphy, s.v. "Penitential Psalms," *New Catholic Encyclopedia*, vol. 11 (New York: McGraw-Hill, 1967) 85–86.

8. James T. Burtchaell, "An Ancient Gift, A Thing of Joy," *Notre Dame Magazine* 14:4 (Winter 1985/86) 14–22.

9. Langdon Gilkey, "Symbols, Meaning, and the Divine Presence," *Theological Studies* 35 (1974) 252.

10. John R. Roach, "Are Christians Free?" *Penance and Reconciliation in the Mission of the Church* (Washington: United States Catholic Conference, 1984) 31–32.

11. Rose Hoover, "Openness of Heart and the Sacrament of Penance: A New Look at Integrity," *Chicago Studies* 25:2 (August, 1986) 222.

12. Joseph Bernardin, "Proposal for a New Rite of Penance," *Penance and Reconciliation in the Mission of the Church* (Washington: United States Catholic Conference, 1984) 41–44.

13. See, for example, "General Sacramental Absolution: Questions," *Newsletter of the Bishops' Committee on the Liturgy* 12 (1976) 82.

The Future of Reconciliation in the Church: Learning a New Art

PATRICK R. COONEY

My presentation is divided into three parts: (1) my understanding of reconciliation; (2) observations on the current situation; (3) challenges for the future.

UNDERSTANDING RECONCILIATION

When you hear the words "sacrament of reconciliation," what do you think? What images come into your imagination? I want to share my image through a story.

Let your imagination take you to a land across the sea and to a time long ago. The valley is encircled by rugged mountains that rise steeply above the tree line. A tranquil river flows through the valley. In the valley, along the river bank, is a village—an unusual village, as you will see.

One day a stranger came into the valley. Shortly after his arrival, he committed a crime. Unfortunately for him, the people of the village had an unusual code. He was put on trial at the village center. Everyone was present. The elder described the crime and the evidence. The stranger was convicted. Before pronouncing the sentence, the elder addressed the people. "Is there anyone among you who will claim this stranger and undergo punishment for him so that he will not be executed?"

Silence. No one stepped forward. Tara broke the spell. "I claim the stranger and submit myself to the punishment on his behalf." The elder, and indeed the whole population, was shocked. "Tara," he said, "you are old enough to know what this means. You will not be executed, but you will suffer the punishment of being left alone by the whole community. You will be left to depend on this stranger for everything you need in life. Should he fail you, no one will come to your rescue. I ask you to reconsider." There was silence. Again it was broken by Tara, who restated her intention.

So it was to be. Tara was separated from the community. No one was permitted to visit her or to help her. She had to depend on the stranger for everything.

But everything went well. The stranger appreciated having his life saved. He was happy to support Tara. He fixed a place for her to live; he brought her food and clothing. He spent time with her every day.

The months went by. The visits became less frequent, the food more meager, the companionship less cheerful. Finally there were no visits, no food, and no companionship. Tara grew ill. Her health continued to deteriorate. She was at the point of death.

Then something happened to the stranger. Perhaps he was threatened; perhaps he felt guilty; perhaps it was something else less defined. He returned to the caring of Tara and succeeded in nursing her back to health. He had changed—he now cared.

To make a long story short, the care blossomed into

love. Tara and the stranger were married. Their life together was blissful. Everything was going right.

Then one day another stranger came into the village.
Unfortunately, he also committed a crime. In the midst
of the people he, too, was convicted. Just as before, the
elder asked, "Is there anyone among you who will claim
this stranger and undergo punishment for him so that he
will not be executed?" Silence. Tara nudged her husband.
He was startled at the look in her eyes. "You expect me
to stand in his place?"

"Doesn't it seem the thing to do?" she replied. "Your
life was saved, shouldn't you save his?" The story ends.

The drama of the new stranger, Tara, and her husband is analagous to the drama of a sinful Church and the
Lord Jesus approaching a cross. One truth is stated. Forgiveness is never merely the erasing of a fault—it is always
a transformation. It involves the forgiven becoming the
forgiver. It involves the passage to new life. Tara's question, "Shouldn't you save his?" is the existential restatement of the Lord's words "Do this in memory of me" and
the re-echoing of "Forgive us our trespasses as we forgive
those who trespass against us."

The sacrament of reconciliation is about all this and
more. It is worship in the midst of which the Risen Lord,
through the Church, takes from his people their stony
hearts and gives them a heart of flesh—redeemed flesh.
The sacrament is for the Church living in her members
a moment of redemption. It deserves our attention.

OBSERVATIONS ON THE CURRENT SITUATION

My observations regarding the current situation of the
sacrament of reconciliation can be listed under eight points.

1) In August 1960 I was assigned to St. Catherine's Parish. Each Saturday the three priests went to their respective confessionals for the assigned hours. The corps of penitents frequented the sacrament at least biweekly. Later I was reassigned. In the second parish most penitents frequented the sacraments every six weeks or two months. Later I was assigned as pastor. I would go to the room of reconciliation and wait the whole period without a penitent approaching. On a big day two penitents came.

My experience as a confessor fits in with the general experience of others. For whatever reason, the faithful do not celebrate the individual rite of reconciliation frequently.

2) The non-use of the Rite for the Communal Celebration of Reconciliation with Individual Confession and Absolution is even more depressing. I would judge that it has almost disappeared from the practice of the faithful. Where it has not disappeared, the rite itself has been modified so that it is a communal preparation for the individual rite. That is something significantly different than what was envisioned.

3) The Rite of Communal Celebration of Reconciliation with General Absolution is celebrated rather infrequently throughout the country and perhaps only in certain regions. Where it has been celebrated, especially in the seasons of Advent and Lent, the participation of the faithful is numerically significant, and if we are to believe the testimony of those who participate, the intensity of the involvement is spiritually significant.

4) The Rite for Reconciliation of Individual Penitents, as fully outlined in the ritual books, has not been used all that frequently. This is a sweeping generalization, but it

is based on conversations with confessors and penitents. Their testimony indicates that this rite, in the actual circumstance of the here and now, is in most cases the preconciliar rite with a changed absolution prayer.

5) Tensions exist about the implementation of first confession prior to first communion. The proponents of both practices are strong in their positions. Unless further study and observation resolve the impasse, this tension will remain.

6) The practice of "devotional confession" continues to be a topic of conversation. There are two perceptions operative. On one hand, those who promote the practice speak of penitents who have a deep consciousness of the call to holiness and are striving. Such a person sees his/her sinfulness in very vivid perspective and in a meaningful way seeks reconciliation with the Church in order to grow. On the other hand, those who are against the practice see the actual penitent differently. They speak of penitents who regularly recite a list of minor faults in a robotic manner which gives no credence that they appreciate their own sinful condition or are humanely involved in the sacrament. This double perception continues among us today. It can have a harmful effect on the place of the sacrament of reconciliation within the life of the faithful.

7) Complaints are made against the Rite for the Communal Celebration of Reconciliation with Individual Confession and Absolution by both penitents and pastors. On the part of the penitent, the complaint is length. When the congregation is large, there are rarely sufficient confessors to hear the confessions with the necessary care within a relatively brief time. Consequently, people react negatively to the longer wait. From the experience of pas-

tors, it is difficult to obtain the services of sufficient confessors. This does not happen because of bad will but rather because of the scarcity of priests in certain areas.

8) The Rite for the Communal Celebration of Reconciliation with General Absolution is surrounded by tensions. The perception that this rite will perhaps become more restricted in the future is a current topic of conversation. A common, generally accepted interpretation of the conditions necessary for such a celebration is lacking. This is more fundamental. Lastly, a personal problem. I am against the mentality that uses the rote recitation of sins for the purpose of absolution in the individual rite. I think that is a poor use of the sacrament. I wonder whether the celebrations with general absolution do not in practice often promote this mentality.

CHALLENGES FOR THE FUTURE

What is the future of the sacrament of reconciliation? Is there a future? I believe that there is. Our task is to make the critical choice of choosing a way to proceed to ensure that future. Where do we begin?

Many years ago I witnessed the marriage of Mike and Sue. The relationship has continued. Often I see them working on a family project. This past spring I was invited to share in their beautification project. Actually it meant cleaning up after the winter and planting flowers. Mike and Sue's seven children were there to help.

On the appointed day I arrived, bringing with me the needed packets of flower seeds. Eileen, the five-year-old, and I were teamed and sent to the side of the house to work. In the process I gave a packet of seeds to her. We got down to work cleaning, picking out stones, raking and preparing the dirt. Finally we were ready to plant. Eileen insisted that we use her packet of seeds, so the package was opened and she gave me one seed to plant. I put it in the prepared hole and started to cover the hole with dirt. "Stop," she yelled. Before I knew what was happening, she knelt down, dug up the seed, ran into the house, washed it off, dried it, and put it back into the packet. I was stunned, but continued to plant.

In time the flowers began to appear. Eileen was fascinated. When she saw the flowers growing, she went to her room, got her packet of seeds, and planted them. With a special joy she watched them grow.

For me, the lesson was basic. If you want flowers, prepare the soil. I believe that the same truth is operable now. If we want a future for the sacrament, we better prepare the ground.

There are, as I see it, at least ten challenges that we can address:

1) *The challenge to preach and teach a living notion of Church.* I am amazed by what I perceive as a dichotomy between what we say theologically about the Church and how we live it. My experience indicates that although our language may be ecclesial, our actual living is more in the context of "me and Jesus." The reality of sacrament logically has no real significance for the "me and Jesus" mentality. Real significance for any sacrament demands a vibrant ecclesial reality, the ground out of which the sacraments come. This ecclesial reality, the Church, is more than an aggregate of members; it must have a shape and a form, it must live and act. It is this Church that we are by the merciful miracle of God. We the faithful must be formed

in this reality. This formation will be done only with great difficulty because it is too countercultural. You and I live in a world that worships individuality. This individuality is so strong that some political theorists doubt that we have the ability to be a nation in the political arena. You can see what this means for a people striving to be a Church.

We need the realization that the Church is not a static club to which one is adjoined, but it is the person of Christ living in his people made one that continues the work of salvation, the building of the Kingdom, and the calling of all creation to its final destiny. This is not a new concept; it has been with us for a long time. We are not always conscious of this reality that we are with Christ and with one another.

The reality and vitality of sacraments are in proportion to the realized and lived ecclesial reality.

2) *The challenge to preach and teach that the Church is called to holiness.* This theme is borrowed from Vatican II. The Church, the Body of Christ, the Lord in his members, is constantly in quest of holiness, not as an end but as a means of proclaiming the mystery of God and building his Kingdom. This holiness is more than abstaining from bad acts; it is the ongoing shaping of the Church's life in the pattern of the gospel, in the pattern of the Lord. Through the sacraments of initiation we have committed ourselves to being the holiness of the Church, which is possible because of the Spirit who is with the Church and with each of the faithful. Together as one we take upon ourselves the responsibility of being this holiness. To fail is to make the Church less than it would have been. This is sin. Out of sin comes alienation from the Church. Out of alienation comes the need for conversion and forgiveness.

When conversion and forgiveness are present, then comes reconciliation.

3) *The challenge to be conscious that our lives are lived in processes.* This is true whether we are talking about holiness or sin or reconciliation. We must acknowledge that processes take place in time and need time. For instance, in the quest for holiness we perceive, we analyze, we judge, we choose, we do. The same can be said of sin. It does not just happen. We perceive, we analyze, we judge, we choose, we do. Sin develops in a recognizable pattern or process that demands time.

The same can be said about reconciliation. We recognize a failure in being the holiness of the Church. We own the failure, are moved to sorrow by the power of the Spirit, regret and turn from it to the Lord God made visible in the Church, and seek forgiveness. The Church, acting in the pattern of her Head, forgives and reconciles. We accept reconciliation, and in that act recognize it as gift and celebrate it.

Too often we act as if all these realities happen instantaneously, and we underestimate the investment of the person in each step of the process. This investment of the person is so critical that without it the acts by themselves run the risk of being less than human. The consciousness of this truth has not always been central to our understanding, much less to our planning.

4) *The challenge to become aware of the different means of reconciliation.* Explicitly, as far back as Tertullian and the Council of Trent and as recent as contemporary writings, we know that reconciliation takes place through fasting, prayer, works of charity, almsgiving, Eucharist, and the sacrament of reconciliation. All the faithful ought

to know this and incorporate this truth into the pattern of their life. Such an awareness gives us the opportunity of seeking forgiveness upon the recognition of sin. This awareness sees the sacrament of reconciliation in its relationship to our life as Church. Among all these ways in which we are reconciled, penance significantly signs our ecclesial reality. It speaks to the richness of our life together in Christ and of the joys of reconciliation that are ours. On the other hand, when we are forgetful of these other ways, the sacrament is expected to bear more than it probably should and hence becomes misunderstood, misdirected, and misused by some.

5) *The challenge to develop a greater awareness of the need for symbolism and ritual in our ecclesial life.* A first-grade child races home from school, dashes into the house yelling, "Mom, I'm home," then runs with outstretched hands into her waiting arms. Is that such a bad reality that we feel compelled to suppress it, deny it, or destroy it? For the mother and child that mutual hug is an action that condenses the cherished happenings of their relationship and makes them present. It is more real than real. It is not childish. It is human-redeemed human. All of us need it if we are to be able to celebrate—even to celebrate sacraments.

The need points to a direction that involves the whole human person. It involves all the cherished happenings that have brought us to this moment. We need to be freed to find and use those condensed actions that speak to us of our being Church.

6) *The challenge to attain a greater clarity about sin.* Sin is part of the ground out of which forgiveness and reconciliation arise. If we deny sin, there is no forgiveness

or reconciliation. But have our presentations on sin always been clear? I don't think so. There have always been two temptations. The first is the temptation to equate sin with human imperfection and rules of human order. We can all build our own caricatures. Yet this still goes on in our adult world.

A second temptation is the reticence to name certain actions and omissions as sins. We all know adult Catholics who easily name trivial items as sins but fail to see the capital sins in their lives. Continuing development in Church living demands that we be as realistic as possible in recognizing sin. After all, the first movement in the process toward reconciliation is the recognition and ownership of our sins.

7) *The challenge to develop our understanding of "communal" in regard to reconciliation.* We talk a great deal about the communal nature of sacraments. Ritually, our application is confusing. In the RCIA process we call the Holy Saturday celebration of the sacraments communal. We point to the faithful who have gathered to celebrate with the elect. The Church is visibly present in its members. Now look at the rites of reconciliation. When reconciliation is celebrated, even using forms two and three, there is no presence of the faithful as faithful who have come to be Church through praying for or receiving the penitents into the community. This representation is left entirely to the confessor.

This is a real challenge. If we believe that the sacraments are communal in the sense of ecclesial, and if we believe that signs, symbols, and rituals ought to be appropriate to the context, we have much work to do. This applies to all three current rites.

8) *The challenge to develop an order of penitents.* Within the near future we will develop a form of the order of penitents. My conviction that this will happen is based on three separate pastoral experiences. The first is quite simple. While I was a pastor, one of our leading active members went through a phase of disenchantment with the Church. His absence from the community was notable. When the young man returned to the community, he felt it necessary to address himself to the total worshiping body both in reference to his being alienated and to his request to be readmitted by the community. While this was not strictly a "confessional matter," it did illustrate to me that there is a need.

The second experience was somewhat different. I had received a telephone call from a young couple who wished to have their union witnessed in the Catholic Church. The young man was Catholic, the young lady was not. Through the preparation period I sensed the growth in faith of the young man. Just prior to the marriage he requested the sacrament of reconciliation. While every effort was made to use the revised rite for the individual penitent in the best manner possible, both he and I felt that something was lacking. Something of a community nature was needed so that he could be restored to active membership. The individual rite in itself did not fulfill that need.

The third experience was completely different. In the Archdiocese of Detroit we are fortunate to have one parish, St. Ephrem, Sterling Heights, that already has an operational order of penitents. The Department of Worship of the diocese asked this parish to put on a workshop for interested parishes. At the end of the day-long program, the participants were able to ask questions of the presenters. A very strongly worded comment was made to the effect that lay people would not tolerate such an order of penitents. Fortunately the adult lay people who presented the workshop had themselves gone through the order of penitents. They spoke strongly of the need for it, of lay people's willingness to participate in it, and of the positive value that they knew as a consequence of being part of the order.

This is one area that certainly needs investigation and development. It is possible within the current guidelines, but it does demand dedication and a great deal of hard work on the part of parish staffs. Obviously, the order would not be intended for everyone who recognized serious sin in their own life and, consequently, alienation from the Church. But it would be extremely helpful to some who have either publicly left the Church or who have just slipped away from active membership. I have found that the people who have been directly involved have found it to be very satisfying spiritually.

9) *The challenge to develop and use penitential rituals.* The use of non-sacramental penitential rituals is another challenge to be considered. Currently one hears very little about these ceremonies being used in any parish, but this type of rite could be extremely appropriate. Such ceremonies present opportunities for focusing the gospel message on contemporary aspects of life that need a Christian scrutiny. The parish would be offering a structure to help in the spiritual development of its people, to evoke a consciousness of sin in areas that perhaps have never been touched, and to lead to sorrow and reconciliation. Such communal penance ceremonies are reconciling in their nature, though not sacramental. Such ceremonies do not vio-

late the canons of Church discipline, since they are non-sacramental and make no claim to fulfill the responsibility of penitents who are conscious of serious sin to submit themselves to the sacrament. Finally, such rituals would be an opportunity to address the hurts involved.

10) *The challenge to have the patience and undertake the study that will be needed.* The liturgical movement in America is only about fifty years old. Much of that time has been spent on questions dealing wtih Eucharist. Other questions necessarily were put on the back burner. As time goes on, the other liturgical topics get their turn. We have seen that happen with baptism, confirmation, and the RCIA. The changes called for come slowly. Note that the RCIA was published in 1972, and even now, after all the efforts, its implementation is just starting.

The sacrament of penance is, in a sense, the new kid on the block. There are tensions still with us from days long past. There are a multiplicity of perceptions that sometimes clash. More scholarship is needed. Certainly for liturgists this is frustrating, but the situation is not hopeless. Remember, immediately after the publication of the Constitution on the Liturgy, we were told that the Eucharistic Prayer would never be in the vernacular. But it did happen.

The sacrament of reconciliation will also have its era. Our challenge is to prepare for that era by turning the ground so that it will be ready for spring. How and when will it come? Let me answer with a story.

On a hill outside a little hamlet in Russia stood an old monastery housing an abbot and twenty monks. Just outside the gate at the bottom of the hill was a house in which a rabbi lived.

The abbot and the rabbi were close friends. Regularly the abbot left the monastery to visit his friend. Over the years the rabbi had become renowned for his holiness. No one knew it better than the abbot.

One evening while they were in conversation, the rabbi told the abbot that he had had a vision in which God told him that he, God, was going to visit the monastery. Naturally the abbot was skeptical, but the rabbi was insistent that it would happen as God had said.

The abbot brought the message to his monks. They were less skeptical. After all, the rabbi was a holy person— if he said it, it would happen.

The monks got down to business. The monastery was dirty, certainly not worthy of God's visit. The next day all the monks worked, and the monastery was spotless.

At chapter that night, a monk suggested that God might come in the disguise of a beggar or a poor person. From that moment on, everyone who came to the monastery was treated like a visiting monarch. The monks just couldn't do more, and they were so gracious in the doing.

Another monk suggested that the prayer life of the community left much to be desired. He felt badly because God might join them in prayer when he visited. The prayer life changed. The monks came on time. They even stayed awake. The chanting became more and more melodic. The ministers took their roles seriously.

Talk started going around. "Have you been to the monastery lately. What a change! It's so clean. The monks have become very generous—no one in need is ever turned away. They pray like angels. It seems that God must have visited them."

In the story, my friends, we find the answer.

CONTRIBUTORS

DR. DORIS DONNELLY is Co-Director of the Center for Spirituality at Saint Mary's College, South Bend, Indiana. She is the author of two dozen articles on the subject of reconciliation and forgiveness. She is the mother of a son, Christopher, and a daughter, Peggy.

REV. KEVIN W. IRWIN, a priest of the Archdiocese of New York, is Associate Professor of Liturgy and Sacramental Theology at The Catholic University of America, Washington. He is active in parish liturgical work and has written several books on liturgy and sacraments, including *Advent-Christmas: A Guide to the Eucharist and Hours*, published by Pueblo Publishing Company, 1986.

KATHLEEN HUGHES, R.S.C.J., is Associate Professor of Liturgy at the Catholic Theological Union at Chicago and a member of the Department of Word and Worship. She has authored many articles and reviews in leading periodicals, and has given many seminars, lectures, and workshops for dioceses, parishes, and religious committees. She has also participated in continuing education programs in Europe and the United States.

MOST REVEREND PATRICK R. COONEY is Auxiliary Bishop of the Archdiocese of Detroit, where he had served as Director of the Department of Worship. He is a member of the Bishops' Committee on the Liturgy.